ETERN
DANCE
OF
LOVE

ETERNAL
DANCE
OF
LOVE

P R O L O G U E

Krishna reveals Himself in the *Bhagavad Gita* as the Lord of All and invites all to surrender to Him and be His personal friend. He promises to look after us through all eternity.

'Surrender to Me and do not fear.' These are Krishna's last words.

Lord Chaitanya came to demonstrate how to surrender to Krishna. There is no difference between the message of Sri Chaitanya and the message of Lord Krishna. ∼

When Sri Chaitanya was travelling in South India he met a simple man who each morning did his best to recite the *Bhagavad Gita* in Sanskrit, though he could neither pronounce the words nor understand them. Chaitanya saw his eyes were filled with tears.

'Why are you crying?'

'I am trying to chant Krishna's words because my guru told me to, but I cannot understand them. As I chant I see beautiful Krishna, so kind to his friend that he has taken the reins of his chariot and is teaching him. This image fills my mind and I can think of nothing else.'

'You are the one who truly understands the *Gita*,' said Chaitanya and embraced him.

The man cried in astonishment, for before him he saw the very same Krishna whom he daily worshipped. ～

revised and expanded edition published by
Fitzrovia Press 2021

originally published as Birth of Kirtan
by Mandala Publishing 2012

Fitzrovia Press
Glastonbury, England
www.fitzroviapress.co.uk

ISBN 978-1-8383222-1-2

Printed and bound by Short Run Press Limited
in Exeter, Devon EX2 7LW
typeset in Centaur 12.5 pt on Munken 80gsm Bookwove,
from forests managed to FSC® standards and other controlled sources

FITZROVIAPRESS.CO.UK

THE BEAUTIFUL STORY OF
LORD CHAITANYA

ETERNAL
DANCE
OF
LOVE

retold from the sixteenth century Bengali sources:
Sri Caitanya Caritamrita by Krishnadasa Kaviraja Goswami
translation and commentary by His Divine Grace A.C. Bhaktivedanta Swami
and
Sri Caitanya Bhagavata by Vrindavana Dasa Thakur
translated by Kusakratha dasa

by
RANCHOR PRIME

Who gave the world pure love for Krishna
1486-1534

Hare Krishna
Hare Krishna
Krishna Krishna
Hare Hare
Hare Rama
Hare Rama
Rama Rama
Hare Hare

Glory to the chanting of Krishna's name,
which cleanses the dust of years from the mirror of the heart,
extinguishes the blazing fire of birth and death,
spreads the shining moon of good fortune
and inspires true wisdom.
This chanting expands the ocean of bliss,
and gives all who bathe in that ocean
a taste of sweetest nectar at every step.

Sikshastaka verse 1

CONTENTS

THANK YOU

I long dreamed of writing this story.
It was my good fortune that in the year 2000 my
friend Raoul Goff (Ramdas) commissioned me to
write the story, published in 2012 by Mandala in
America under the title *The Birth of Kirtan*.

In the years since, I rewrote extended and refined my original text.
My thanks to my daughter Annie Prime for her professional editing
and appendices, to my proofreader Sita Thakurani, to my agent
Susan Mears for backing me during the long gestation of this book,
and to my friend Kishor for his helpful insights. Special thanks to
Anjana for her last-minute fine tuning, and for bringing me to the
feet of Gopal in a loving home in Glastonbury. 🌿

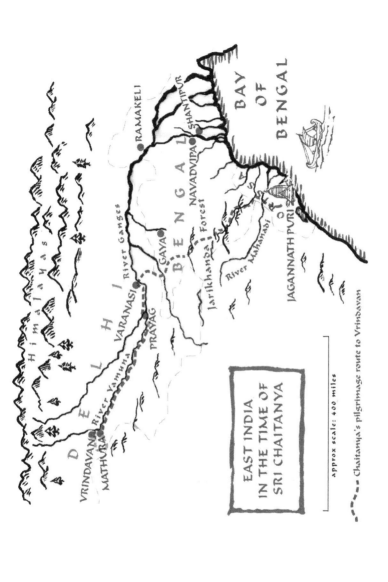

Himalayas

VRINDAVAN
MATHURA

D E L H I

River Yamuna

River Ganges

VARANASI

PRAYAG

GAYA

RAMAKELI

SHANTIPUR

NAVADVIPA

Jarikhanda Forest

B E N G A L

River Mahanadi

JAGANNATH PURI

BAY
OF
BENGAL

EAST INDIA
IN THE TIME OF
SRI CHAITANYA

approx scale: 400 miles

- - - - Chaitanya's pilgrimage route to Vrindavan

Introduction

GOLDEN MOON

SRI KRISHNA CHAITANYA was that rare one whose life was his message. He wrote no books, organised no mission, had few direct disciples and only lived on Earth for forty-eight years. In his adult life he became fully detached from the world and virtually his only form of public teaching was to sing the names of God. In his final years he withdrew to a mystical seclusion away from all but his closest companions. Yet during his brief time on Earth he planted the seeds of a spiritual movement both inner and outer that five hundred years later sends waves around the world. His life was truly a demonstration of the ultimate power of love.

The message of Chaitanya was simple: look for those devoted to the service of Krishna and with them hear about Krishna and chant Krishna's names. By so doing your love will grow and you will find lasting happiness. He shared his innermost secrets of the highest reality with a handful of close companions who preserved them for posterity in

Sanskrit poetry inscribed on palm leaves. Those confidential teachings are revealed on the inner plane of the heart through the blessings of Divine Love. Until the dawn of the twentieth century Chaitanya and his teachings were unknown outside India, and would have remained so were it not for my beloved master. It was foretold that one day Lord Chaitanya's name would be known in every town and village, and so it is coming to pass. In these urgent times of planetary renewal and transformation his story is at last being heard around the world.

Sri Chaitanya was born in Navadvip, West Bengal, in the year 1486 and disappeared in 1534. He spent his last years in Puri, the great temple town of Orissa on the east coast of India. He taught the path of devotion to Krishna and shared his love with hundreds of thousands. During his lifetime he was known as Gaurachandra (golden moon), Gauranga (golden one), Nimai (born under a neem tree), Vishvambhar (sustainer of the world), Mahaprabhu (great master) and Krishna Chaitanya (living spirit of Krishna).

From an early age he showed miraculous powers that persuaded many close to him that he was a divine being. Although in public he always denied this, his followers worship him to this day as the incarnation of Krishna.

THE MYSTERY OF SRI CHAITANYA

HIS LIFE IS A PARADOX. Tradition tells us he revealed his divine identity to a few favoured devotees, yet on each occasion swore them to secrecy. He showed a natural humility, his personal habits were simple and modest, yet he was one of the most exuberant religious figures of his time. He urged his followers not to try to see Krishna, but instead to feel Krishna's mystical absence in this earthly realm by embracing feelings of divine separation. He expressed these feelings in his prayer:

> *'A moment seems like a thousand years, tears flow from my eyes like torrents of rain, all the world appears vacant without you, Govinda.'*

Krishna is as near as a heartbeat, yet hidden from his creation. Sri Chaitanya lived in a perpetual state of divine longing, his emotions often swept into ecstatic states. We are told he possessed extraordinary charisma and a physical beauty that overwhelmed all who met him. He was exceptionally tall, broad-shouldered and long-armed, with large lotus-shaped eyes. His complexion was described as *gaura*, golden, and he often manifested a glowing effulgence. He was a powerful scholar and teacher, quick-witted, with a deep and penetrating voice. Wherever he went he left an indelible impression.

Sri Chaitanya's longing to see Krishna, his deep feeling of separation from his beloved, was the same as the love of the gopis for Krishna. They were the cowherd girls of the forest of Vrindavan, and in the spiritual sky they are Krishna's eternal companions. Stories tell us how, in their youth, Krishna and the gopis had intense loving affairs; during the day they played in the forest and at night they danced under the moonlight. These stories inspired some of India's most memorable literature, art, music and drama. After Krishna left Vrindavan He never returned. He and the gopis spent the rest of their lives remembering the love they shared in their youth. The essence of this constant remembrance is found in the love between Krishna and the gopi Radha. Her love for Krishna is the supreme display of the longing for God that lives in the heart of every soul. This longing was the theme of Chaitanya's life.

His biographer, Krishnadas Kaviraj, based his work on journals kept by Chaitanya's closest companions. His epic biographical poem *Sri Chaitanya Charitamrita* (1615), completed in his old age, is one of the great masterpieces of Bengali literature. The poet poured a lifetime of devotion and learning into his work and captured the mystical spirit of Chaitanya's life and teachings.

Krishnadas opens by telling us the identity and significance of Sri Chaitanya. The following pages summarise the poet's prologue.

THE VAISHNAVA FAITH

THE ANCIENT VAISHNAVA FAITH into which Chaitanya was born taught that God, Vishnu, is the supreme maintainer of all life. Vishnu manifests in three ways: as the all-pervading spirit that is the basis of all existence, as the Inner Guide living in the hearts of all, and as the Original Supreme Person who is love personified and exists both within and beyond this world. These three aspects of God—pure energy, guiding presence and personification of love—coexist eternally.

God appears to our earthly vision in unlimited forms, like the countless waves of the ocean. These forms illuminate the world as candles light up the darkness. The one original candle from whom these many candles emanate is Krishna. This Original One came to Earth as Lord Chaitanya.

KRISHNA'S INCARNATION AS CHAITANYA

CHAITANYA SAW KRISHNA everywhere and in everyone; he spoke constantly about Krishna; he sang Krishna's names and prayed to Krishna ceaselessly. He was the embodiment of love for Krishna. The poet Krishnadas tells us Krishna came into this world as Chaitanya for three reasons—three profound desires that brought him to live among us here on Earth.

His first reason was to bring people together to chant Krishna's names. Wherever he went Chaitanya taught this simple practice as the best means to overcome illusion and uncover our soul's natural love. In this age of confusion and adversity when life is so difficult, he taught us simply to sing the names of God.

His second reason was to share his love. Krishna radiates pure love, a love that flows perpetually between Him and the goddess Radha. She is the personification of love and she is never separate from Krishna. Their love expands to fill all creation. All existence is the dance of the love between

Radha and Krishna. To reveal their love to all beings Radha and Krishna united in the divine being of Sri Chaitanya.

His third and secret reason for incarnation was Krishna's intense desire to become Radha. The Goddess Radha enchants Krishna and her spirit inspires the whole creation. Longing to experience Radha's unique being, Krishna chose to be her, to be one who loves Krishna just as she does. To accomplish this, Krishna in the form of Chaitanya experienced the spirit of Radha in three distinct ways. He tasted the joy of her love; He appreciated his own beauty as only she can; and he experienced the ecstasy that is hers in being loved by him. In these ways Chaitanya was none other than Radha and Krishna combined. To understand this secret of Chaitanya's identity is possible only by the blessings of his intimate companions, says the poet Krishnadas.

NITYANANDA, BROTHER TO CHAITANYA

CHIEF AMONG THOSE close companions, like a brother, was Nityananda. Born in East Bengal around 1474, he served Chaitanya as his principle representative, carrying his teachings to the people of Bengal. He shone bright together with his beloved Chaitanya. These two, Gaura and Nitai, like the sun and moon, rose to light up the darkness of the world. They illuminated the hearts of their devotees, dissolved their shadows and awakened them to love of God.

Chaitanya was Krishna and Nityananda was Balarama. In the eternal world of spirit Balarama is Krishna's older brother, who loves to care for Krishna and to play with him.

While Krishna enjoys with his friends, Balarama expands to become Vishnu and to manifest the material worlds. First He creates countless universes then He enters these worlds of matter to support them in multifarious divine incarnations. Vishnu is the source from whom all creation flows, the one who enters the hearts of all as Inner Guide, and who cares for the created worlds. As the one who cares for the world and all within it, Balarama is full of kindness and mercy for those caught in these mortal worlds. He is pure unconditional love and the original guru of all.

Nityananda, as the personification of Balarama, reaches out to us all and calls us back to Krishna. So wrote the poet Krishnadas.

ADVAITA, WHO PREPARED THE WAY

THE NEXT CLOSE COMPANION was Advaita. Born fifty-two years before Chaitanya, he was a respected elder of the Vaishnava community. The poet identified him as an incarnation of Vishnu; yet Advaita saw himself as one who serves others. Despite his advanced age (he lived for more than a hundred years), Advaita shared with Nityananda the mood of service to Chaitanya. The joy of service, wrote the poet, is a thousand times greater than the joy of merging with God. Loving service is the mood of all in creation— whether they play the role of elder, friend, or lover—service brings them unlimited happiness.

'I am servant of Sri Chaitanya and servant of his servants,' sang Advaita. This joyful song of service is the song of all creation. Those who aspire to absolute oneness with God do not know the ecstasy of loving service. Even Krishna wants to taste this emotion of loving service, and so He descends in the form of Chaitanya.

ONENESS IN DIVERSITY

KRISHNA CAME TO EARTH as Chaitanya, but he did not come alone. He brought with him a host of companions to act alongside him in his human drama. These companions were born across Bengal and Orissa, and gradually assembled in Navadvip where they prayed for the appearance of Krishna. As well as Nityananda and Advaita was Gadadhara, who was Chaitanya's lifelong friend and confidante, and Shrivas, whose humble wisdom and love showed an example for all to follow.

The message of love for Krishna was embodied in these five persons united in a single truth. Krishnadas called them *Pancha Tattva*, five truths: named Chaitanya, Nityananda, Advaita, Gadadhara and Shrivas. These five danced, sang, laughed and cried, sending forth waves of love that transformed Hindu society in Eastern India in the early sixteenth century.

Devotees of Chaitanya invoke the presence of the fivefold *Pancha Tattva* by calling on their names with this mantra:

sri krishna chaitanya prabhu nityananda
sri advaita gadadhara srivas adi gaura bhakta vrinda

In Chaitanya's day India was alive with philosophical debate. The Sanskrit literatures, particularly the *Vedanta Sutra*, *Upanishads*, and *Bhagavad Gita*, were sources for endless exploration of nature, the soul and God. Two themes lay at the heart of Vedanta philosophy: *Advaita* and *Dvaita*— oneness and difference. Chaitanya's ecstatic religion of Krishna Consciousness was founded on both of these; its essence was love guided by philosophy and common sense. His teachings emerged in a series of encounters with learned teachers during his travels around India. His words, recorded for posterity by his direct disciples, have been passed down through generations of teachers.

Chaitanya's philosophy came to be known as *achintya-bhedabheda*, meaning 'inconceivable oneness and difference.' This describes the relationship between the soul and God. Some teachers proclaim oneness; others proclaim difference. Chaitanya proclaimed both. He said all living beings are one with God yet simultaneously each of us has our own unique and eternal individuality and is different from God. We are one in quality, as a drop of water is one with the ocean—in essence the drop and the ocean are one—but we are different in quantity: the drop is tiny while the ocean is vast; we are one with God in our essence, but God is infinite and we are infinitesimal. God is master of the entire cosmos, whereas we cannot even be masters of our own body and mind. If we choose, we can lose our individuality in the vast ocean of God's being. This merging is called liberation or *moksha*, and is the goal of the teaching of non-duality known as *Advaita*.

Yet we have another choice: to pass through the oneness, awaken our eternal individuality and enter Krishna's endless play of divine love, far beyond this temporary world of birth and death. This fulfils our limitless potential to be eternal loving companions of God. Instead of losing ourselves in the nameless and formless ocean of *brahman* we can discover ourselves in the everlasting and ever flowing ocean of *premananda*, bliss and love. This was Chaitanya's wish—for us to realise our eternal identity as lovers of Krishna, and be recipients of Krishna's love throughout eternity. This eternal dance of love is what he came to give us.

Some speak of God as Creator, some as Soul of the World, some as the universal Onenesss, some as Inner Guide, some as Vishnu, some as Rama, some as Shiva, some as Goddess, some as Holy Trinity, some as Christ, some as Allah and some as Jehovah. These countless aspects of God or Goddess are revealed to each of us according to our desire to receive and according to our inspiration. All these divine visions can be found in the inspiration and wisdom channeled by Lord Chaitanya.

DEEPENING LEVELS OF PRACTICE

WE CAN FIND INSPIRATION in Chaitanya's life and teachings in each of the three moods of his incarnation. For instance, we can experience the divine sound of God's names by sharing in the many ways of singing or dancing together, or by practicing solitary meditation on the vibration of the mantras through chanting softly on prayer beads, a practice called *japa*. Either or both of these ways is a spiritual path complete in itself. They are further enriched by another kind of hearing—when we hear the words and teachings of the holy books shared among friends or from the mouth of a teacher linked to the succession of teachers who embody the chain of devotion.

Hearing and chanting the sacred names in the company of others will draw us to the next stage, which is when we enter a regular practice of devotional service under the guidance of a guru. This stage is called *sadhana*, or practice. In time this leads us to taste the sweetness of Krishna's love as revealed in God's infinite creation, in the hearts of those around us, and ultimately within our own hearts where Krishna eternally speaks to us.

For those most fortunate comes entrance into the deep mysteries of the love and spiritual emotions of Radha and Krishna, of Goddess and God, shared in the eternal luminous reality of pure spirit in the everlasting transcendental realm beyond this mortal world. We can enter this reality even whilst sitting here on Earth.

All these devoted practitioners find life's perfection. Sri Chaitanya calls us all to our eternal spiritual home.

THE CHAIN OF DEVOTION

THE STORY OF LORD CHAITANYA and his teachings has been carried since his time on a wave of wisdom and love down to the present day. It passed through the hearts of innumerable devotees, transmitted through an unbroken chain of teachers. This chain of devotion and wisdom was brought to the West by Chaitanya's empowered devotee, my guru Bhaktivedanta Swami, known to his followers as Srila Prabhupada. In 1969 he established a beautiful temple hidden away near the British Museum in Bloomsbury, London, and dedicated it to Radha and Krishna.

As a young art student I walked into that sacred place and heard Prabhupada's message delivered by his young disciples. I was captivated, and within a few days I too became a follower of Chaitanya and of his faithful teacher Srila Prabhupada. The following year I met Prabhupada and he initiated me as his disciple.

Chaitanya's life cannot be told as an ordinary history or biography. It is a mystical and mysterious tale, as recorded by his contemporaries and set into sublime poetry. My guides in finding the authentic history of Chaitanya are two sixteenth-century Bengali poets and philosophers, Krishnadas Kaviraj Goswami and Vrindavan Das Thakur. This book is based on their accounts. My guru Srila Prabhupada blessed me with the opportunity to tell this story, which he gave the world in the 1970s in an elaborate translation and commentary that filled many volumes laden with devotion and poetic wisdom. I am here to pass on its essence to a new audience.

Our world is going through changes as never before. Hearts and minds are opening to receive fresh inspiration. Please forgive my limitations, for I am just a messenger. Chaitanya is not of this world. Though once he lived and breathed here he belongs to another plane of reality. Hear his story with open mind and heart and you will be drawn into his eternal dance of love.

Ranchor Prime
Radhastami
14 September 2021

Book One

HOME

I

DIVINE CHILD

IN THE SPRING OF 1486, as the full moon rose into a total eclipse above Bengal, a golden child was born. He was to be known as Gaurachandra—Golden Moon.

His story began with Advaita, the one who prepared the way. People called him Acharya, teacher. His mission was to call Krishna to appear on Earth. He saw the condition of the world around him and prayed for divine help. In answer to Advaita's prayers Krishna descended from the spiritual world and was born in Navadvip. So the poets tell us.

Advaita lived in the village of Shantipur. The fields around his village were flat and fertile, watered by the Ganges and her tributaries in the populous land of Nadia. The district was dominated by the town of Navadvip, on the bank of the Ganges a hundred and fifty miles inland from the Bay of Bengal. Navadvip was a prosperous and cultured place, famed as a centre of learning. All day teachers gathered beside bathing places lining the sacred river. There they taught the intricacies of logic and Sanskrit grammar. By evening, the town came alive with amusements and celebrations in praise of the Goddess.

Advaita Acharya had a town house in Navadvip, where he was the senior teacher of his community. In his main home in the nearby village of Shantipur he organised regular prayer meetings for local Vaishnavas, whose tradition was in decline. People were losing interest in the Vaishnava faith.

Vaishnavism upheld an ordered life centred around Vishnu, maintainer of the worlds. Vishnu was worshipped as the source of all, who presided over the gods and goddesses of the higher realms. Advaita saw that people's attention in Navadvip was shifting away from Vishnu, toward elaborate worship of the goddess Durga. Along with this he saw an increasing pursuit of worldly happiness. He knew that material pleasures would not satisfy the inner longings of the soul, whereas devotion to Vishnu could bring people the peace and happiness they sought. Every day he prayed for help to bring change, asking Krishna to descend among the people and teach them a better way.

Advaita was friendly with a gentle brahmin named Jagannath Misra. He had moved from East Bengal to settle in Navadvip where he married Sachidevi, daughter of a local teacher. Their life together had not been easy; Sachi bore eight daughters, but each of them had died soon after birth. Despite her prolonged struggle she never lost faith in the Lord, and continually prayed with her husband for at least one healthy child. At last their prayers were answered when their ninth child was born a strong and healthy boy, whom they named Vishvarup. His arrival filled them with happiness.

Soon after, Sachi conceived again. This time she felt the spirit of God descend upon her, and in her joy she radiated spiritual beauty. After their succession of misfortunes, it seemed now, with one strong child and a second one on the way, their fortunes were changing.

Friends stopped Jagannath on the street to congratulate him and offer him gifts. In Sachi's dreams she saw angels singing prayers to the child in her womb. Both of them were sure a special child was to be born.

That evening the moon entered a full eclipse and a smoky twilight enveloped the world. During this time of shadows, people had been taught to fear the darkened rays of the moon, believing they brought misfortune. To counteract this they sought the all-embracing shelter of Mother Ganges, immersing themselves in her sacred waters to sing God's names and offer prayers. Even those not normally observant took these precautions, and such was the influence of this ancient custom that with one voice people all over Bengal were chanting the names of God. So it was, with the world in shadow and Krishna's names vibrating everywhere, that the golden son of Sachi was born.

Advaita saw the eclipse and knew in his heart something special was occurring and that his prayers were being answered. He too bathed in the Ganges and chanted with joy. The Vaishnavas saw that he was celebrating more than just a lunar eclipse. They didn't fully understand, but they joined in his chanting.

Everywhere the atmosphere grew peaceful and calm. People's minds were uplifted. Musicians played musical instruments; in the streets were dancing and joyful singing; in the sky some saw celestial beings and heard music vibrating through the heavens.

As soon as his son was born, Jagannath Misra called his family priests to chant prayers with musicians to accompany them. Crowds came with gifts to honour Sachi and her newborn child. Chief among them was Sita, wife of Advaita Acharya. She came from Shantipur bringing bracelets, necklaces, silks, sandalwood and gold coins. She knew this child had come in answer to her husband's prayers.

THE STREAM OF FRIENDS and relatives visiting mother and child noticed something surprising. Whenever Nimai started to cry, he would fall silent and smile blissfully as soon as they chanted Krishna's names. If they stopped singing, however, he again began to cry. They soon realised that he wanted them to sing God's names ceaselessly, and this they gladly did, clapping their hands and filling the air with the sound of 'Hari, Hari!' As they chanted, the women saw the child shining with a golden light, so they named him Gaurahari, Golden Lord.

Strange things happened around the house. Visitors saw ethereal presences in the shadows or peering through the windows. Some feared they were malign spirits, others thought they were divine beings come to honour the child. Uncertain what was happening, people guarded the house with their prayers and sang Krishna's names all the more.

At the name-giving ceremony, Sachi's father, Nilambara Chakravarti, calculated his grandson's horoscope.

'This child has deep intelligence and will become a great scholar,' pronounced Nilambara. 'He will be a ruler of unimaginable glory. Perhaps he is the brahmin, long foretold by our people, who is to become the saviour of Bengal.'

The horoscope predicted that the child would teach the path of truth, bringing good fortune to everyone around him. Because it appeared that he would bless the whole world, Nilambara gave his grandson the name Vishvambhar, meaning 'Protector of the World.' And since he was born under a neem tree, which has the reputation of driving away harmful spirits and whose leaves heal infections, his mother called him Nimai. This became his childhood name among his family and friends.

After the name-giving came the traditional choosing of gifts by the infant, intended to reveal his calling in life. Three offerings were spread before baby Nimai: a tantalising plate of sweets and puffed rice, a glittering mound of coins, and the holy book *Srimad Bhagavatam* laid on a cloth. Guests gathered round to see which gift he would choose. To everyone's delight, he took hold of the *Bhagavatam* without hesitation and embraced it to his heart. The ladies sang Krishna's names in joy, and as they did so little Nimai danced in their laps.

Time passed and Nimai began to crawl around the house. About his waist was a belt with tiny bells that tinkled as he moved.

While he was playing in the courtyard, one day a large cobra emerged from the bushes and coiled itself around him. Nimai wasn't afraid. He played with it and laid among its coils, gurgling with delight. His mother came into the courtyard and rushed forward crying in alarm, at which the snake uncoiled itself and glided harmlessly away. Nimai wanted to crawl after it, but she scooped him up and carried him to safety, while the snake disappeared and was not seen again. Everyone believed he had been rescued from certain death.

Soon Nimai started to walk. Mischievous and full of curiosity, he entered neighbours' houses and crept into their kitchens, where he ate their food and drank their milk. Sometimes he broke their clay pots. However when the women caught him, which they were sure to do, he pleaded with them so charmingly that they laughed and let him go.

Spellbound by this beautiful child, his mother and father believed he must be a divine being. His shining face was bordered by curling locks, his eyes large like the petals of a lotus, and his smile captivating. When they saw Nimai, people spontaneously offered gifts such as bananas or ornaments, even those meeting him for the first time. He used these gifts as bribes to make everyone sing Krishna's names. This game went on until all his family and friends were chanting the names of God. When they did so he laughed and danced, and when they did not he wept. So all came under his influence.

One day, decorated with jewels, Nimai was playing outside his home. Unnoticed, he wandered off in the direction of the Ganges. When he was out of sight of his house two thieves came upon him, saw his shining ornaments and could not believe their luck.

'This child is a treasure trove, let's kidnap him and steal his jewels.' They enticed Nimai with sweets.

'Oh, little boy, you look lost. Come with us and we will carry you home.' One of them lifted Nimai onto his shoulders.

'Yes,' Nimai laughed playfully, 'please take me home.'

Off they ran with their precious burden, searching for a hiding place. Nimai was enjoying the ride, but at home his absence had been noticed. All were frantically calling his name.

On ran the thieves, turning this way and that, until they thought they were far from from Nimai's home. They set him down and were about to strip him of his jewels when they realised they had travelled in a circle and arrived right back in front of Nimai's house. His father saw them and gratefully picked up his little boy. He was about to thank the two strangers when they fled in panic.

Everyone wanted to know where Nimai had been and what had happened to him. He spoke kindly of the foolish thieves.

'I wanted to go to the Ganges, father, but I got lost,' he said sweetly. 'Then those two nice men carried me home.' Jagannath again wanted to thank the strange men, but they could not be found and were never seen again.

LITTLE NIMAI RAN about the house, captivating his parents' hearts as they delighted in watching his energetic explorations. One day Jagannath Misra, sitting down to study his books, called his son.

'Nimai, bring me the *Bhagavatam*.'

Nimai scampered over to where the sacred book was kept and struggled to lift it in his small arms. As he watched his obedient son stagger toward him with the weighty volume, Jagannath distinctly heard the tinkling of ankle bells coming from Nimai. Sachi heard the sound too and looked round with curiosity. Nimai wore no ankle bells that either of them could see. Yet they both clearly heard this musical sound.

Later they saw another curious sign. Nimai had gone out to play and Sachi was busy cleaning. She was about to sweep the floor when she noticed small footprints everywhere. These were no ordinary prints, for they showed the unmistakable marks of Krishna's feet. The soles of Krishna's feet are renowned for bearing the marks of flag, thunderbolt, fish and lotus flower. She saw these marks all across the floor, but could not bring herself to believe that her son had made them. She called Jagannath and together they wondered how these divine footprints could have appeared. The only explanation they could think of was that their Vishnu deity, whom they prayed to daily, had come to life and blessed their home. Excitedly they called Nimai to show him the wonder.

'Vishnu himself must have descended from our shrine and secretly walked around our home to bless us,' said Sachi, 'and as he walked his ankle bells tinkled.'

Nimai looked at the footprints he had left in the dust and simply smiled.

A pilgrim entered Navadvip on his way through Bengal. He was a retired brahmin who had dedicated himself to visiting all the holy places of India. Around his neck he carried a small deity of Bala Gopala, baby Krishna, whom he worshipped every day. The brahmin had renounced the world and no longer had a home. Wherever he was he felt at peace, confident in the Lord's protection and looked after by the kindness of people he met on the road. Jagannath Misra met him in the marketplace and invited him to stay in his house.

'It would be an honour for us if you would cook for Gopala in our house.'

The pilgrim agreed to this invitation, and Jagannath brought him home. He gave him a place for worship and thoroughly cleaned the cooking area, providing grains, fresh vegetables, milk and ghee with which to cook. When midday arrived a beautifully prepared meal was ready and the pilgrim began to offer it to Bala Gopala.

The pilgrim placed his offering before his deity of baby Krishna and sat down to recite prayers, calling Krishna to come and eat. As soon as he started chanting the mantras, little Nimai entered the room as if in answer to the pilgrim's call and began to help himself to the food on the altar.

'Stop!' cried the pilgrim, 'You have spoiled my offering.'

Jagannath heard his cry and hurried into the room. He saw his mischievous son eating and chased him away.

'Don't be angry with the child,' said the pilgrim. 'Bring me whatever ingredients you have left and I will cook again.'

Jagannath was pacified and took the boy to a neighbour's house where he had him carefully watched while the pilgrim cooked a second time. By late afternoon he was ready to make another offering. As he began to chant his prayers Nimai somehow escaped from the watchful eyes of the women next door and appeared smiling and eating with great satisfaction. The pilgrim called out in distress.

'Help! This boy has come again to spoil my offering.'

This time the devoted brahmin was worried he must have done something to offend his Lord.

'Krishna does not want my offering,' he lamented. 'Today I must fast.'

Jagannath was mortified that this misfortune should befall the pilgrim for a second time when he was an honoured guest in his house, and he threatened to punish little Nimai.

'What good will your punishment do?' admonished the pilgrim. 'He is only a child and should not be blamed. I will just have to accept Krishna's will.'

Just then Nimai's older brother Vishvarup arrived home from school and was amused to learn of his behaviour.

Vishvarup's presence calmed everyone as it always did, and soon he persuaded the pilgrim to cook a third time. More provisions were brought and Nimai was taken away yet again. This time he was secured in another room with his mother and put to bed. All was calm and soon Nimai fell deep asleep.

With daylight fading, the pilgrim settled down to cook. As night fell the adults became sleepy. One by one they went to bed and closed their eyes. Alone in the flickering light of a lamp, the pilgrim prepared to make his offering. This time, while making heartfelt prayers for Krishna to accept his offering, he slipped into a deep trance, contemplating the form of his beloved Bala Gopala.

In the darkness Nimai stirred. Soundlessly he slipped from the bedroom and came in answer to the pilgrim's prayers. The pilgrim opened his eyes and saw before him the very same Krishna of his meditations. In his hand Krishna clutched butter and rice which he was tasting, and from his neck swung a garland of forest flowers. The fortunate pilgrim saw surrounding Krishna the eternal forest of Vrindavan, in which cows grazed peacefully and birds called from the branches of trees. Gazing upon this vision he could not check his tears as he shivered in ecstasy. He fainted, and when he came to he saw Nimai before him.

'I have shown you this vision of myself because for many lifetimes you have been my faithful devotee,' spoke Nimai. 'You were once a guest of my father Nanda Maharaja in Vrindavan. At that time the same thing happened and I ate your offering. Now I am living here in Navadvip. I will show everyone my favour by blessing them with love for God. You may stay in Navadvip and see me regularly, but you must tell no one of what you have seen and heard tonight—this will remain our secret.'

The pilgrim found himself alone again in the room. In silent ecstasy he ate the food blessed by Nimai, then slept soundly.

Afterwards he became a regular visitor to Nimai's house. He never left Navadvip, and his story remained a secret until many years had passed.

WHEN NIMAI WAS OLD ENOUGH to begin school a ceremony marked his passage into boyhood. The custom was to cut a boy's hair, chant verses from the Vedic hymns and introduce him to writing the letters of the Sanskrit alphabet. Jagannath gave his son a slate and a piece of chalk and guided his hand to form the letters of the alphabet for the first time. As he did so he pronounced each letter, '*ka, kha, ga, gha,*' and Nimai repeated the sounds after him.

Nimai took delight in making the sounds and learning how to write each letter. Within two or three days he had mastered the whole alphabet. Day and night he wrote out the names of God, chanting as he did so.

'Rama, Krishna, Hari, Murari, Mukunda.'

So began Nimai's schooling. He quickly made friends with his classmates and soon became their leader. He was high-spirited and loved to start disputes, which he always won. Wherever he was there was sure to be trouble, and he gained a reputation as a naughty boy. Yet, far from his unruly behaviour making him unpopular, everyone loved him all the more.

Sometimes, when he could not have what he wanted, Nimai became frustrated. He tried to catch birds but they always flew away. He longed to touch the moon and stars, demanding 'Give, give!' and crying inconsolably when he could not reach them.

At such times someone would sing Krishna's names and others would follow, dancing and clapping. Then Nimai would be happy again.

One afternoon after school Nimai was by the Ganges playing with his friends. Every day the brahmins of Navadvip gathered there to chant mantras and perform their rituals. He loved to tease them. He threw dust over them so they would have to wash themselves in the river, and while they were in the water he splashed them. The more they forbade him the more he ignored their protests. Finally they lost patience and a group came to complain to his father.

'Jagannath Misra, please do something about your son. When we chant our mantras to Vishnu he interrupts us and claims he is Vishnu. He takes our offerings meant for Vishnu, and says, "Why are you troubled? I'm the one you worship." We try to catch him, but he escapes into the water where he floats for hours with his friends, splashing us if we come near. You must discipline your child.' They spoke as if they were angry, but really they loved Nimai and did not want him to come to any harm.

The village girls were often by the Ganges, and they too were the object of Nimai's teasing. Some of them complained to his mother.

'Mother Sachi, your son insults us and splashes us, and steals our clothes while we are bathing. When we make offerings of flowers and fruits he spoils them and after we finish bathing and are all clean he throws sand over us. None of us like him. Please stop him or we will report him to our parents.' Although they said this, the girls loved Nimai.

Hearing such complaints, Jagannath took his stick and set off for the riverside, determined to deal with his disobedient son.

This made the girls sorry, and they ran ahead to warn Nimai. He made his friends promise to say they had not seen him at the Ganges that day, then ran off. By the time his father arrived he was nowhere to be seen.

'Nimai didn't come today,' his friends chorused. 'He must have gone straight home from school by the other path.'

The brahmins were more truthful but they also spoke up for Nimai.

'We saw him here, but he ran away in fear,' they said. 'Don't be angry with him, Jagannath—just give him a good talking to. We all love him really, and we think you are truly fortunate to have such a son.'

Saying this the brahmins embraced Jagannath and pacified him so that, feeling reassured, he returned to his house. Just as he got there Nimai arrived home, apparently from school, covered in dust, carrying his school books, his fingers stained with ink.

'Mother,' he cried, 'I have been working hard at school all day. Now I need to go down to the Ganges and bathe.' Jagannath looked with surprise.

'What are you up to Nimai? Everyone at the Ganges is upset with you.'

'Father, they make up stories about me,' Nimai complained. 'I haven't even been to the Ganges today.'

Smiling and not waiting for an answer, the boy ran off laughing to join his friends by the river, where they gathered round to praise his bold escape.

At home his parents were left bewildered.

'Surely all these people would not lie about Nimai,' reasoned Jagannath. 'Yet he can't have bathed already. His hair was dry, and dust and ink stains covered his body. Who is this child of ours, who at once enchants and maddens everyone? He must be someone special. Perhaps Krishna himself has been born among us.'

Speaking like this, their hearts overflowing with love, Jagannath and Sachi felt endless bliss.

2

BESIDE THE GANGES

NIMAI GREW IN CONFIDENCE and authority. Though still only a young schoolboy he would listen to no one—not to his teacher, nor to his mother, nor even to his father. But one person commanded his respect—his older brother Vishvarup, to whom Nimai was devoted. Vishvarup possessed a natural authority and at the same time a gentle nature that made him loved and respected by all. He was always studying the *Srimad Bhagavatam*, which tells the complete story and philosophy of Krishna, and regularly gave discourses on spiritual topics.

One day Vishvarup visited Advaita's house in Navadvip where the Vaishnavas were gathered to hear about Krishna. Despite his youth, Vishvarup was addressing the assembly, who were all attracted by his learned devotion and his explanations of spiritual life. Absorbed in talking about Krishna and enjoying the spiritual company, he forgot to return home for supper. Meanwhile his mother waited for him.

'Go and fetch your brother,' she told Nimai. The young boy ran off to bring his older brother home, arriving breathless and excited at Advaita's house.

'Mother wants you to come home and eat,' exclaimed Nimai, tugging at his brother's clothes. He did not notice that he had become the centre of attention. The Vaishnavas had heard about Nimai but not seen him. Now he was before them they were struck by this child's presence. They wondered what it was about him that captivated them so. It never occurred to them that he might be Krishna, soul of souls, the very one they daily heard about and prayed to.

On this occasion Vishvarup obediently accompanied Nimai home, but increasingly he spent time away in the company of devotees. He wanted only to hear about Krishna, and family life held no attraction for him. Even when he was at home, he confined himself to the shrine room and was rarely to be seen.

When he was twelve, Vishvarup overheard his parents planning his marriage. This filled him with dismay. He had but one desire—to devote himself entirely to God. Marriage held no attraction for him. He lay awake that night wondering what to do. Finally he decided to become a wandering monk. The very next morning he left home and travelled to South India, where he spent the remainder of his life on perpetual pilgrimage from one holy place to another.

Sachi and Jagannath were distraught. Day and night they wept, and could not be consoled. Nimai, who had been devoted to his older brother, was deeply affected. His hero and inspiration had abandoned him and gone off to be a sadhu. This experience made an indelible impression on his young heart, and he resolved that one day he would follow in his brother's footsteps. However he understood that for now his parents needed him more than ever, and he must take Vishvarup's place at home. He would become serious about his studies, he decided, and abandon his mischievous play.

Nimai threw himself into his schoolwork. So sharp was his intellect that once hearing a verse from any text he remembered it by heart. His learning rapidly increased until no one could defeat him in debate.

'Jagannath Misra, you are a lucky man to have such a gifted son,' people told his father. But now a new fear took root in Jagannath's heart. Suppose Nimai learned all the scriptures as Vishvarup had, would he not reach the same conclusion—that family life was an illusion—and leave home to follow his brother? To everyone's dismay, Jagannath forbade his son to study.

'Without being educated how will our boy earn a living?' protested Sachi. 'No one will want their daughter to marry him.'

'Being well educated has not earned me much of a living,' responded Jagannath. 'We are poor, and have to rely on wealthy men who are themselves without education. Krishna will look after Nimai as he looks after us all.'

Nimai obeyed his father, but with nothing to do he was bored. He returned to his mischievous ways, teasing girls, fighting boys, and playing pranks on the grown-ups. Soon everyone was begging Jagannath to let his son study again.

'You are lucky to have a son who wants to study,' they said, 'You should be encouraging him, not holding him back.'

Jagannath relented and accepted their advice. A ceremony was held in which he offered his son the sacred thread, symbol of second birth as a brahmin who studies spiritual knowledge, and he enrolled him as a student of the learned teacher Gangadas Pandit. Nimai was happy again and became inseparable from his books. He told his father not to worry that he would leave home like his brother: he would be a dutiful son and look after his parents.

One day Nimai had a dream. His brother Vishvarup took him by the hand and led him away, telling him to become a sannyasi just as he had done. In his dream Nimai protested, 'Our parents are helpless without me. I must stay and serve them.' So Vishvarup sent him back home with messages of love for their mother. When he awoke Nimai told her of his dream.

Jagannath also had a dream. He saw his beloved Nimai grown into an adult with shaven head and dressed as a sannyasi. Around him were thousands of followers whom he led in singing Krishna's names while passing through many towns and villages. Jagannath's heart overflowed with joy to see his son so loved and absorbed in divine service, but at the same time he was anxious. When he awoke he prayed fervently to Lord Krishna.

'Please protect our son, Lord, and do not take him from us. We are your servants, and whatever we have is yours.'

Soon after this the saintly Jagannath Misra, in whose home Krishna secretly played as a child, was taken from this world. His community gathered on the bank of the Ganges to cremate his body. As they watched his ashes merge with the river, Nimai and Sachi wept.

In the coming years Nimai never left his mother's side. As she watched over him constantly, she gazed at his moonlike face and forgot her grief.

SACHI'S ENTIRE WORLD revolved around Nimai. She gave him everything he asked for. Nimai tried to settle down as a devoted son and dedicated student, but sometimes he became restless. His father had known how to control him, and his elder brother had been his inspiration and confidential friend. Now they were both gone he missed their reassuring presence. There were times when Nimai's frustrations boiled over, when his mother simply could not do enough.

It was Nimai's custom each day to take a garland of flowers to offer Mother Ganges in worship before bathing in her sacred waters. One day, as usual, he asked Sachi for the garland.

'Just wait and I will bring it to you,' she replied.

When he heard her say, 'just wait,' Nimai lost patience. The sorrow and frustration stored in his heart since the death of his father burst forth, and he was overcome by a sudden rage. He ran inside the house in a reckless mood and began to pull things off shelves. Clay pots stood in a row, holding Ganges water, milk, oil, ghee, salt and spices. He smashed them all. When he ran out of containers to break, he ripped open sacks of rice, flour and grains, and scattered their contents on the floor. He tore apart clothes, until every garment was in tatters. Still his rage was not quenched, so he turned upon the house itself. Wielding a heavy stick, he beat the fragile mud and bamboo structure and tore at its thatched roof.

Soon the house was reduced to ruins and all within destroyed. Nimai threw himself upon the ground and began rolling and beating the earth, crying hot tears. His terrified mother, at a safe distance, could only watch him roll in the dirt, until at last, his anger spent, exhausted and soaked in tears, he fell asleep stretched out upon the bare earth. To Sachi he appeared beautiful. Timidly she stepped forward, and while he slept she massaged his body, gently wiping away his tears and cleansing the dust from his skin. Then at last she brought the garland and laid it beside him.

After some time Nimai opened his eyes and saw the garland. He smiled at Sachi. After the passing of a terrible storm, the sun had returned. He picked himself up, took the garland, and without a word walked to the Ganges. While he was gone, Sachi cleared a space and using supplies borrowed from her neighbours, she cooked their lunch. Nimai returned and ate in silence. Without a word he gathered together his books and left for school, where he spent the remainder of the day with his class friends as if nothing had happened.

At the end of the day Nimai came home and called his mother.

'Mother dear, take this and restore everything.' He pressed into her hands two gold coins. 'Krishna provides all our needs,' he said. 'We will never want for anything.' Without further explanation he went to bed.

Sachi could not understand why her son had behaved as he did, nor where he acquired the gold. Whatever he did she accepted, as Mother Earth tolerates her children. Cautiously she took the coins and showed them to her friends. Receiving their assurances, she spent them to restore their house and replace everything as it had been before.

At school Nimai surpassed everyone in his studies of Sanskrit grammar and logic. Although he was the youngest of Gangadas's students, he was soon able to defeat in argument even the senior pupil Murari Gupta. Navadvip teemed with students of the various academies. When each day ended they congregated by the Ganges and played games, splashing and fighting in the water, challenging each other in verbal contests, always vying to see who was the strongest or cleverest. Nimai knew no fear. Without hesitation he would go up to a group of older boys and challenge them to a dispute.

'Why are you so arrogant and always picking fights?' they demanded to know. 'Do you think you are better than us?'

'Ask me any question and see,' laughed Nimai. And so they would try to catch him out. But none could. First he would perfectly explain some particular point in a way no one could refute, then he would take the opposite position and disprove his own argument. In this way he baffled them and was victorious even among his elders. Yet none of them minded being defeated. Instead they embraced him and made him their leader.

Nimai was an unusually beautiful youth with black curling hair and deep smiling eyes. He walked with power and grace so that, when he passed by, people would be transfixed. Soon he was surrounded by friends and admirers, but he never spoke of his future mission. Who would understand? People were preoccupied with materialism and not interested to hear about Krishna.

Only the Vaishnavas who met at Advaita's house would listen to him. They were outnumbered and misunderstood; people mocked them for their constant singing of Krishna's names and thought they were sentimental fools; but Advaita encouraged them.

'Don't despair. I feel in my heart that Krishna will help us.' In response they loudly sang the names of Krishna, 'Hari! Hari!'

Nimai, nearby with his friends, happened to hear the name of Hari and came running to Advaita's house.

'Why have you come, my child?' asked the adults.

'Why did you call me?' responded Nimai, laughing.

No one understood his words, and he ran off to play again with his friends.

MARRIAGE BECKONED. At the age of sixteen Nimai was now head of his household, with the responsibility to care for his mother. Custom required a young man in his position to have a wife. Wishing to fulfil his duty, Nimai began to think of finding a partner.

One day on the way home from school he met Laksmidevi, daughter of a local brahmin named Vallabha Acharya. They were each following the path along the bank of the Ganges when they came face to face.

This was not their first encounter. When he was a boy, Nimai used to delight in teasing the girls by the river. Sometimes they collected flowers and fruits to offer to the goddess Durga, praying for her help in finding future husbands. At these times Nimai would tease them and disrupt their worship.

Among them was a girl he thought special. She came only once to pray for a husband, and although they were both still young children, a bond formed between them that day.

'Worship me, and I promise I will fulfil all your desires,' Nimai had told her, and she had devotedly given him all her offerings intended for Durga. She never came again. That girl was Laksmidevi.

Now on the path by the Ganges they met again, and smiled in recognition. Love awakened in their hearts, and they accepted one another as partners.

In the brahmin community of Navadvip was a match-maker named Vanamali. He always had his ear to the ground and knew who was ready to be married. His heart told him to speak with Sachi about her son.

'I know of a suitable match for Nimai. Her name is Laksmidevi, daughter of Vallabha Acharya.'

Sachi was hesitant. Although she knew her son must now become a grown-up householder, she didn't want to lose her Nimai. So after listening to Vanamali she sent him away without an answer. Nimai, however, heard that the matchmaker had visited, and was pleased. He spoke to his mother, encouraging her to call him again. Once Sachi knew Nimai's mind, her hesitation was gone. She told Vanamali to make the arrangements without delay. In time-honoured fashion the matchmaker called on Laksmidevi's father, Vallabha, and greeted him with respect.

'The son of the noble Jagannath Misra, whose name is Vishvambhar, is a gifted and saintly young man. He would be an excellent husband for your daughter Laksmidevi. What do you say?'

Vallabha was overjoyed at this suggestion, but one thing troubled him.

'I am embarrassed that I can't afford a dowry. All I can give are fruits and flowers. Please ask Sachi if this is acceptable.'

Sachi was not in the least deterred at hearing of Vallabha's modest circumstances. It mattered only that he was a good man and happy for his daughter to marry her son. So the marriage was agreed and an auspicious date set according to astrological calculations.

On the eve of the great day they held a ceremony at Nimai's house, with the bride's parents present. They chanted prayers and offered a garland to the groom, while musicians and dancers entertained their guests.

Early next morning, while last-minute preparations were under way, the whole neighbourhood gathered to celebrate the marriage of their much-loved Nimai. As the auspicious hour of sunset approached, Nimai, dressed in new cloth and decorated with a fresh garland, accompanied his mother to Vallabha Acharya's house. Vallabha received his son-in-law with respect, offered him a seat, and then presented Laksmidevi to him. While everyone chanted the names of Krishna, the bride walked around her husband seven times and prayed to Vishnu for his future health and happiness. Then they held hands and were worshipped by the whole assembly. All felt themselves floating in an ocean of joy.

That night the couple stayed at the bride's house, attended by her girlfriends, and the next day Nimai brought his wife home, where further festivities were held. The couple had such an aura of beauty and grace that people thought they were witnessing Vishnu and his eternal consort the goddess Laksmi herself.

THE NEWLY MARRIED COUPLE settled down, watched over by Sachi. Nimai's home life took on a gentler mood with Laksmidevi by his side. She bestowed light and comfort all around her. Sometimes Sachi fancied she saw a glowing flame next to her son, then looking again saw Laksmidevi. At other times she smelled the aroma of fresh lotus flowers pervading the house. She thought this girl must indeed be the Goddess of Fortune, come to live with her and her son, and this was why they no longer experienced poverty.

Nimai regularly withdrew in silence to the shrine room, and when he did Sachi heard celestial flute music and saw supernatural light spilling from the doorway to fill the house. Sometimes she heard heavenly singing and the tinkling bells of unseen dancers, or she glimpsed luminous figures entering her home to pay homage. At these times she shivered and her eyes glistened with tears.

In scholarship Nimai surpassed all others. He had long overtaken his fellow older pupils, and even his teachers could not better his knowledge of Sanskrit grammar. A well-to-do citizen of Navadvip named Mukunda-Sanjaya requested Nimai to teach his son. Nimai readily agreed, and this led to others also wanting to become Nimai's students. One was Murari Gupta, who had been a school-friend of Nimai's. The two of them used to enjoy debating points of grammar, and although Murari was older and more educated, Nimai always won their debates. Now Murari was a doctor, and he wanted to learn Sanskrit, so he approached Nimai.

'Vishvambhar, please let me be your student,' he submitted, and Nimai happily agreed.

Soon other students asked if they too could join Nimai's classes. One of them was Mukunda, another former school-friend. He was a gentle soul who loved to sing at the Vaishnava gatherings at Advaita's house. When he sang to Krishna the devotees would openly cry. Beside being Krishna's devotee, Mukunda was an accomplished scholar, and proud of his learning.

If Nimai encountered Mukunda on the street, he would challenge him to a debate on some point of philosophy. Each time this occurred Mukunda tried to overcome Nimai, but only got humiliated. Eventually, if he saw Nimai approaching he would run in the opposite direction, until one day Nimai cornered Mukunda and took him by the hand.

'Why do you avoid me? Is it because I never speak of Krishna?' Saying this Nimai turned to his friends and proclaimed, 'I promise you the time will soon come when I will speak of nothing but Krishna.' From that day Mukunda became his student.

Another of Nimai's friends who asked to be his student was Gadadhara. The two of them became close companions, and remained close for the rest of their lives.

Seeing all these students joining Nimai, the wealthy Mukunda-Sanjaya offered his spacious courtyard at the front of his house as a teaching place. So it was that Nimai began his teaching career. He became Nimai Pandit, and his fame spread as the best Sanskrit teacher in Navadvip.

Between classes Nimai roamed the town with his students, always with a book in his hand. If he met any teachers he challenged them to defeat him in argument. He excelled in all departments of knowledge—grammar, logic, rhetoric and philosophy—and was quick to prove his mastery.

Nimai's behaviour might have seemed arrogant, but he had a way of gaining his opponent's respect. This gave him a strange effect on scholars. They feared his sharp wit and cutting tongue, but they couldn't help being attracted to him. Consequently, although one by one he defeated them all, he made no enemies in Navadvip.

At the end of each day Nimai went to the water's edge. There he sat on the bathing ghats, illuminated by the setting sun and surrounded by students and admirers. All who looked on him wondered at his beauty and learning, while those who were Vaishnavas secretly prayed for him to become a devotee of Krishna and protect them from their critics.

One of Nimai's special friends was a simple banana seller named Kolaveca Shridhar. It was Nimai's sport to tease the shopkeepers, begging their wares to see how much he could talk them into giving him. Laughing, he would go from one stallholder to another in the market place, and invariably walk away with free gifts. Frequently he reached Shridhar's banana stall at the end of the marketplace. Shridhar was a poor man whose main occupation was prayer. He owned a small banana patch and made a meagre living selling his produce, patiently accepting as the blessings of God whatever little he earned at his market stall. Nimai, dressed in fine robes and ornaments, used to make fun of Shridhar's worn clothing and ramshackle home. He always made a point of begging bananas from him, even though he knew Shridhar couldn't afford to give them away. Shridhar didn't mind—he was glad to feed Nimai and gave to him with genuine love. The two of them, although so different, became close friends.

A FAR-SEEING ASTROLOGER visited one day.

'I have heard you know everything. Tell me who I was in my previous birth,' asked Nimai.

The astrologer meditated and saw a vision of Vishnu, the soul of the universe. It seemed to him that the one standing before him was that divine person. At first he was speechless. Nimai waited to hear his conclusion.

'By my calculations,' he finally said, ' in your previous birth you were the shelter of the universe. And you are still that same person.'

When he heard this Nimai smiled.

'You are mistaken. I know that in my last birth I was a cowherd boy, and because I looked after cows I have now been rewarded with birth as a brahmin.'

'Whatever you are, I offer you my respects,' was all the astrologer could say.

3

YOUTHFUL SUCCESS

EARLY EACH MORNING Nimai Pandit met his students in the courtyard in front of Mukunda-Sanjaya's house. Lessons lasted until noon, when they all swam in the Ganges. Nimai then went home to worship Vishnu and have lunch followed by a short nap. In the afternoon, books in hand, he was off to stroll around the town, where he would stop and chat to friends, laughing and joking as admirers gathered round him.

Eventually he made his way to the bathing ghats where he again met his students. Sitting in their midst he was like the moon surrounded by stars. He lectured, first proving a point, then disproving it, then proving it again. People watched and listened in awe. No other pandit could match him.

'Is this a demigod come to live among us?' they said. 'Or an incarnation of Vishnu? We have heard that one day a brahmin will become King of Bengal. Perhaps this is he, for he has all the signs of a king.'

The scene was just like when Krishna sat by the River Yamuna among his cowherd boyfriends, all of them laughing and joking, and looking upon Krishna with love. Just as those cowherd boys felt indescribable happiness, so also did the students who surrounded Nimai Pandit.

One day a famous pandit arrived in Navadvip. He had the title Digvijaya, which means champion. Such was his intellect and learning that he believed himself invincible. Wherever he travelled he challenged scholars to debate, and in the process won considerable wealth. The Digvijaya Pandit paraded into town with a retinue of attendants on horses and elephants.

He issued his challenge. The scholars of Navadvip should put forward someone capable of resisting him in debate, or award him a certificate stating that he had defeated them all. When Nimai Pandit heard this news from his students he smiled to himself, and began to think how to defeat this proud man without causing him too much public humiliation.

'The man himself should not be destroyed, only his pride,' Nimai confided to Gadadhara. 'I will try to meet him privately.'

That evening, as Nimai taught by the Ganges under a full moon, along came Digvijaya Pandit. He had heard of Nimai Pandit and was curious to meet him. Seeing Nimai's striking appearance and hearing him speak, he realised he was in the presence of a rare genius, so he sat quietly at a distance. Nimai saw him and paused. He greeted him respectfully, then invited the champion scholar to entertain them all with some verses in praise of the Ganges. The pandit was unable to resist the invitation to show off his skills. He possessed a special gift: he could spontaneously compose perfect Sanskrit poetry. Without hesitation he stood up, and for three hours glorified the Ganges, chanting Sanskrit verses like the wind and holding his audience spellbound. At last he ended, and Nimai thanked him.

'Your verses are wonderful,' Nimai said graciously. Then he added with a smile, 'But they are difficult for us to understand. Please explain their meaning.'

As soon as the learned man began his response Nimai interrupted.

'One of your verses, however, contained five faults.' He quoted the precise verse and explained the errors, then asked the pandit to elucidate.

Digvijaya Pandit was taken aback. How could Nimai select and remember a single verse from a three-hour discourse? He tried to explain the verse in question, but found himself lost for words, since Nimai had correctly pointed out clear mistakes in both grammar and logic. Embarrassed by this uncharacteristic carelessness, the great man lapsed into an awkward silence.

Some of Nimai's students began to titter, but he quickly silenced them. He had defeated the pandit and had no wish to make a spectacle of him: for such a proud man, public humiliation would be unbearable.

'You must be tired from your journey. Why don't you rest for the night and tomorrow we can meet and discuss everything.'

Digvijaya gladly retreated to his lodgings in thoughtful mood. He was a devoted worshipper of Sarasvati, the Goddess of Learning, and looked upon her as the source of his strength. He must have displeased her, he thought, and that was why she had allowed this defeat by a mere boy. That night when he prayed to Sarasvati as he always did, she appeared to him in a dream.

'The boy who defeated you is Vishnu, master of countless universes. Before Him I am powerless,' spoke the merciful Goddess. 'I am revealing this secret to you because of your sincere devotion to me. Now go quickly and surrender to Him.'

In the morning Digvijaya hurried back to Nimai. He fell at his feet.

'I did not recognise you,' he apologised, humbled now. 'I beg your mercy.'

'Do not talk like this,' protested Nimai. 'You are a great brahmin and have no need to bow before me.'

'The Goddess came to me last night and told me you are Vishnu himself. I only wish that you teach me how to be free from material attachments.'

'The only knowledge truly worth possessing is to understand that Krishna is the source of all happiness, and to know how to serve Him. Abandon your wealth and pride, and surrender to Him,' spoke Nimai. Then he made Digvijaya promise not to reveal to anyone what he had learned about Nimai's true identity. Like others overcome by Nimai in debate, Digvijaya did not grudge his defeat.

His heart was won over and his life transformed. He gave away his elephants and released his servants, so as to travel as a lone mendicant devoted to Krishna.

Following this incident Nimai Pandit's fame spread and he was proclaimed a lion among debaters. But no one knew who he really was.

A VAISHNAVA SANNYASI NAMED ISVARA PURI visited Navadvip. While there he stayed with different families and encouraged them in their devotion. Several times Nimai invited Isvara to eat at his house where they spent long hours talking about Krishna. Isvara was an ecstatic devotee, and whenever he spoke of Krishna his eyes filled with tears. Nimai became affected hearing from him. Once when they were in discussion Isvara corrected Nimai on a point of grammar, and Nimai happily accepted the correction. No one else had ever been able to correct him like this. From that day Nimai looked upon Isvara Puri as his teacher, and both he and Gadadhara shared a love for him.

Another devotee who began to influence Nimai was Shrivas, one of the leading Vaishnavas of Navadvip. He was a friend of Advaita Acharya, and held regular prayer meetings in his house. Shrivas watched Nimai's growing success.

'Why spend your time lecturing and studying books,' he told Nimai. 'These things are vanity. If you are truly learned, you will worship Krishna and teach others to do the same.'

'For a little longer I must carry on my studies,' said Nimai, 'then by your mercy I will become a devotee of Krishna.'

THE TIME CAME FOR NIMAI TO TRAVEL. Frequent comings and goings in the town of Navadvip carried his reputation as a teacher across Bengal. Students came from far afield to study under him, and some of them, after learning his commentaries, took them home and shared them with others. Hearing this, Nimai decided to embark on a teaching tour of East Bengal. Leaving his mother in the care of Laksmidevi, he set off with a group of friends and students.

As he travelled from village to village and people gathered to hear him, his fame grew. Many, attracted by his mesmerising beauty and commanding authority, became his students. During this tour he started teaching people to chant the names of Krishna, as he had first done in his childhood. The impression he created on those who met him left a lasting attachment in their hearts, and many became Vaishnavas.

Among these was a young brahmin named Tapana Misra. He was searching for the truth, but although he had studied many books his heart was not satisfied. In a dream he was told that Nimai Pandit was the person who would enlighten him, so he set off to find him. One day, while Nimai was teaching Sanskrit in the shadow of a banyan tree, Tapana Misra came before him and prostrated himself on the ground, begging Nimai to become his spiritual teacher.

Nimai's students were mostly interested in acquiring a material education, but here Nimai recognised a sincere seeker of the truth, and gave him a clear instruction.

'In this confused age the best spiritual practice is to chant the holy names of Krishna, seek the company of devotees, and together chant Krishna's names. Then your love for God will grow and you will find lasting happiness.'

Tapana Misra was the first to receive Nimai's spiritual teachings. He wanted to join Nimai there and then and return with him to Navadvip, but Nimai had a different idea. Soon he would start his life's mission, and he saw this sincere young brahmin as someone who could help him in the future.

'I want you to go to the holy city of Varanasi,' he told Tapana Misra. 'Settle there with your family and wait for me. I promise I will come there and teach you the goal of life.'

Varanasi, on the banks of the Ganges some five hundred miles upriver, was North India's greatest centre of spiritual learning. It was Nimai's plan one day to visit that city and instruct its religious leaders. Tapana would go ahead to prepare the way. Nimai gave his young disciple a warm embrace, and the two parted.

LAKSMIDEVI AT HOME IN NAVADVIPA missed her husband greatly. Each night she lay awake thinking of her beloved, as her eyes filled with tears. Two months passed without news of his return. Weakened by loss of appetite, desiring only eternal union with her Lord, she lost the will to live without him. She sat beside the Ganges, meditating on Nimai's feet with determination, and left this world behind. Laksmidevi's death was a deep shock to everyone, especially Sachi who was left all alone. Her tears flowed day and night and were pitiful for her friends to behold.

Unaware of these events, Nimai brought his travels to an end and turned homeward. When his newly acquired students heard he was leaving, many of them decided to come with him to continue their studies. So it was that, after two months of travelling and teaching, Nimai returned to Navadvip with a large company, bearing valuable gifts he had collected from the people of East Bengal.

Late one afternoon Nimai and his party arrived home. His friends greeted him with celebration and joy. Some took him to the Ganges, and while he was bathing his mother cooked a feast. As dusk fell they all sat down to eat and exchange stories, with much laughter and joking. None of them knew how to break the news of Laksmidevi's death. When all was over and his friends were taking their leave, Nimai entered his home to greet his mother and his wife. He found only Sachi, weeping.

'Mother, what is wrong—are you not pleased to see me?' She could not answer.

'Where is Laksmidevi?' he cried, and at last a friend broke the news.

'O Nimai, your dear wife went to the Ganges and has not returned.'

When he heard these words Nimai remained motionless and soft tears glided down his golden cheeks. After a while he recollected himself. Recalling the wisdom of the Vedas he embraced his sorrowing mother and consoled her with comforting words.

'By the will of Vishnu we are brought together and imagine ourselves related as sons and mothers, or husbands and wives, and by his will we are again parted. Since it is his wish for the fortunate Laksmidevi to reach the Ganges before her husband, we need not be sad.'

Her son's calm words helped Sachi regain her composure. She still had him, and that was what mattered most. So long as Nimai was with her she could weather any storm. With his support she called their friends and relatives, and together they performed the rites for Laksmidevi's departed soul. In due course, as the sun returns north from his southward journey, happiness returned to their hearts.

BEREFT OF HIS YOUNG WIFE, Nimai threw himself into his teaching work. His inclination toward the spiritual life, and his desire to teach it to others, were a secret confided only to a few trusted friends such Mukunda and Shrivas. Externally he maintained his usual sociable nature with friends and strangers alike. Privately, however, he began to change.

He became strict in his religious observance, for example in his daily worship at home he rose very early and spent hours in prayer and puja, and he expected his students to be strict in theirs too, insisting they wear the sign of Vishnu on their foreheads and give proper attention to their brahminical duties. Another new characteristic was that he no longer joked with girls. As a young boy he had loved to tease them by the Ganges, but from now on he preserved a respectful distance from the girls of Navadvip. This reserve toward women remained a feature of his life ever after.

Sachi saw her son's absorption in his work and knew his heart: he missed Laksmidevi, as did she. After some time had passed she resolved to find him a new wife and see him once more settled in household life. She had noticed a brahmin girl named Vishnupriya who was devoted to the Ganges and respectful to her superiors. She seemed an ideal match for her son. After receiving Nimai's consent, Sachi sent a message to the girl's father, Sanatan Misra, requesting his daughter's hand for Nimai. He was a well-to-do brahmin and gladly accepted the proposal for Nimai to be his son-in-law.

A wealthy man of Navadvip, Buddhimanta Khan, was an admirer of Nimai and offered to sponsor a grand wedding festival.

On the eve of the wedding two celebrations were held, one for Nimai at his home, and one for Vishnupriya at her home. The men and women of the town offered the betrothed their blessings. The many brahmins of Navadvip were showered with gifts and sumptuously fed.

As the wedding day dawned Nimai went to the Ganges

to bathe. During the morning Sachi visited her relatives to offer them gifts of fruit, ghee and grains. All over town houses were decorated with waterpots, flags and mango leaves. In the afternoon Nimai dressed in new yellow cloth, gold earrings, a jewelled necklace and a crown. His face was adorned with sandalwood paste, black eye-ointment and the sign of Vishnu on his forehead.

A grand procession wound through the town toward the bride's house. Nimai was carried by his friends in a palanquin and surrounded by the women of the town singing auspicious mantras. Lamps were carried ahead, followed by dancers, musicians and flag bearers. Children ran alongside laughing and playing, and everyone danced, even the elders of the town. The procession passed along the bank of the Ganges, through the centre of the town, and as the sun was setting, arrived at Sanatan Misra's grand palace. He came out to greet Nimai and took him inside, where the women of the family offered him gifts and worshipped him with lamps.

When all guests were seated with Nimai in the centre, Vishnupriya appeared. She walked around her husband seven times, then offered a garland at his feet, which he in turn placed around her neck. They sat side by side while their guests showered them with flowers. Priests chanted mantras and lit a sacred fire, and a wedding feast was enjoyed by everyone. When all was done the bride and groom retired to spend their first night together as guests in her father's house.

The following day a procession led the couple back through the streets to Nimai's house, with more chanting, music and celebrations. There Nimai distributed gifts to all who had helped, as well as to the poor.

Nimai's wedding to Laksmidevi had been a small family affair. Now, two years later, the whole town turned out to celebrate his wedding to Vishnupriya. He turned to Buddhimanta Khan, whose generosity had paid for it all, and warmly embraced him. Although he was not yet eighteen years old, Nimai Pandit had achieved worldly success and fame, and established himself as the leading scholar of Navadvip. His destiny, however, lay elsewhere.

4

AWAKENING

NIMAI REACHED EIGHTEEN YEARS OLD. Custom required a son to make offerings for the soul of his departed father. So now, being once more happily married, he went on pilgrimage to the great Vishnu temple in Gaya where he would observe the ceremonies. Taking with him some of his students for company, he followed the course of the Ganges upstream from Navadvip.

After several weeks walking from village to village they reached Gaya. Inside a towering great temple was the footprint of Vishnu. To see this footprint was the high point of a pilgrimage to Gaya. Pilgrims passed through the outer precincts of the Vishnu temple, then, attended by priests, they mounted steps to reach the inner shrine room. There, illuminated by burning lamps, surrounded by chanting of mantras and offerings of garlands and incense, was the sacred footprint of Vishnu embedded in a large black stone.

When Nimai gazed at Vishnu's footprint his eyes filled with tears, his body shivered, and he fell to the stone floor in trance. His companions had no idea what to do. This was the first time they had witnessed such a change in Nimai. They helped him to his feet and guided him from the temple.

As he emerged Nimai saw before him the face of Isvara Puri, the teacher who had so impressed him when he visited Navadvip and gave instruction to Nimai and Gadadhara. Without hesitation Nimai prostrated before the devout brahmin then rose to embrace him with tears of affection.

'I came here to pray for the deliverance of my ancestors,' he said. 'Now I have found you, who has the power to deliver us all from birth and death. Please grant me the gift of Krishna's lotus feet.'

'Dear Nimai, surely you yourself must be Krishna,' replied Isvara Puri. 'For since first I saw you I can think only of Him.'

Nimai smiled.

'I am fortunate to find you, my dear friend.'

For the rest of that day the two parted. With his companions Nimai visited the sacred sites of Gaya where he made offerings for his ancestors, then returned a second time to gaze upon Vishnu's footprint. At the end of the day they came back to their lodging where Nimai cooked for them all. He was about to eat when Isvara Puri, filled with love for Krishna, arrived to see him. Nimai insisted on giving him the plate he had kept for himself, then cooked again. When they had both finished eating, Nimai made sure Isvara Puri was comfortable and served him by massaging his feet with fragrant oil.

'Now I have met you and served your feet, my visit to Gaya is successful,' he said.

For some days Nimai stayed on in Gaya in the company of Isvara Puri and considered what to do. Deep spiritual emotions were awakening and he could think of nothing but Krishna's lotus feet. It was time to take an important step. Humbly he approached Isvara Puri and asked for initiation into the chanting of Krishna's name.

'I give my body in your service. Please bless me with love for Krishna,' prayed Nimai.

Isvara Puri took Nimai aside and gave him his mantra, so accepting him as his disciple. The two embraced, crying tears of love. Thus Nimai received initiation. On that day he accepted Isvara Puri as his spiritual master and forever after remained devoted to him. Later in life he always carried with him a small bag of dust taken from Isvara Puri's birthplace, and told his intimate friends that this dust kept him alive.

NIMAI WENT ALONE TO A QUIET PLACE and settled to meditate on the mantra he had been given. As soon as he chanted Krishna's name he entered a deep trance and saw Krishna. When he emerged from his meditation, the vision of Krishna vanished and Nimai cried aloud.

'O Krishna, my dear father. O my life, Lord Hari. Where have you gone?' Falling to the ground in distress he called again and again for Krishna. His students came in search of him and found him crying and rolling in the dust. They were alarmed and did their best to calm him, but he wanted them to leave him alone.

'Go home. I can no longer teach you. I must leave immediately for Vrindavan to find Krishna. He is the master of my life.'

That very night, when they were all asleep, Nimai crept out and started for Vrindavan, Krishna's childhood home, a month's journey to the West. In a state of trance he walked into the night and as he walked he called upon Krishna. After some time a voice responded out of the darkness.

'Now is not the time for you to go to Vrindavan. First you must fulfil your destiny to spread this chanting everywhere and so teach all souls to love God. Go back to Navadvip and show people how to chant Krishna's names. Later, when you have done this, you will be able to visit Vrindavan.'

Hearing this divine voice, Nimai halted and returned to Gaya, where he found his companions. Together they journeyed back the way they had come. As they travelled, day by day his longing for Krishna grew.

One day they passed through a village named after Krishna. There Nimai caught sight of a beautiful boy dancing and playing the flute. He was dark-skinned, dressed in a bright yellow dhoti, and wearing a necklace of jewels, with a peacock feather decorating his dark curling hair. The boy ran up to Nimai and embraced him, then darted away. No one else saw this. Nimai was distraught. He had seen Krishna and felt his touch, but how would he find him again? Absorbed in the memory of this vision and the feel of Krishna's embrace, he continued on until the company entered Navadvip.

NIMAI WAS A CHANGED PERSON. Gone were his youthful arrogance and playful wit. His many friends in Navadvipa, eager to see him after his absence, found in him an air of introspection and an uncharacteristic modesty. He greeted them quietly as they crowded round to hear his news.

'Let me go inside,' he said excusing himself, and with his close companions retreated from the crowd.

Once in his room he told them of the wonders of Gaya, of the great temple and his bliss upon seeing the footprint of Vishnu. But before he could go on to speak of his fortunate meeting with Isvara Puri he was flooded with emotion, weeping helplessly and calling on Krishna. His tears flowed like the Ganges. His friends had not seen him like this before and none of them knew how to respond. After a while he recovered and asked them to let him rest. Tomorrow at Suklambara's house, he said, he would speak to them again.

Next morning Gadadhara and other Vaishnava friends gathered as usual at Shrivas's house. Those who had been with Nimai the night before reported his transformation. When the others heard of his change they celebrated, hoping he would choose to join them and help their cause. Excitedly they made their way to Suklambara's and waited.

Nimai soon arrived and began talking about Krishna. As he spoke he was once more carried away. He said he had found his Lord in Gaya but now he had lost him. He was overcome and fell to the ground. The effect on those with him was unexpected; all were moved by his powerful emotions and found themselves helplessly weeping along with him. After a while Nimai became silent. He sat up and everyone grew still. As he looked around the room his eyes fell upon a familiar face.

'Gadadhara my friend, you are here. You have always been devoted to Krishna. As for me, I wasted my youth. Now at last I have found the treasure of my life, but because of my sins this treasure has left me.' He took Gadadhara's hands in his and appealed, 'Can anyone help me find Krishna, and relieve my distress?'

In turns they all cried and laughed, together chanting Krishna's name, and so passed the whole day.

Word of Nimai's change spread through the small community of Vaishnavas. A wave of hope arose among them. With Nimai their fortunes would change; people would take notice and no longer mock them. Advaita Acharya, their respected elder, encouraged them, saying Nimai's transformation must be the answer to his prayers.

In Nimai's home, however, the mood was different. His mother and wife were alarmed by his sudden change in behaviour. Whenever Vishnupriya tried to speak with him he turned away and called for Krishna. At night he kept them awake with his tears. Sachi, remembering the loss of her first son, feared Nimai too might leave her. Understanding her fear, he sat with her and tried to explain. He taught her, just as the youthful sage Kapila had once taught his mother, of the miseries experienced by the soul trapped in the womb, who calls upon God for release from the pains of birth and of the life to follow.

'Dear mother, this world is full of suffering. The only way to escape the miseries of birth and death is to worship Krishna. Don't you see?'

No matter how he tried to encourage her and explain to her what had happened to him, still she was unhappy. She insisted that he return to his teaching work, and sent him to see his old teacher, Gangadas.

'You have found great fortune,' said Gangadas. 'But your students are waiting. You must teach them.'

Early the following day, in obedience to his teacher, Nimai went to the Ganges to bathe and wait for his students. They came, books in hand, and begged him to resume teaching. He sat with them around him and began to teach, but he found himself unable to talk of anything other than Krishna. He taught them how all scriptures pointed to Krishna; how Krishna's name was found in every word; how devotion to Krishna was life's greatest treasure and all else was a waste of time. They were enthralled by his words, yet bewildered. He broke off, laughing.

'Forget your studies. Today we will bathe in the Ganges.' And there, suffused with a new beauty they were astonished to see, he played with them in the waters as he had always done.

In the days that followed Nimai regularly met his students and taught them, speaking only of Krishna. They questioned him closely, trying to make him return to his old style of teaching, yet whatever they asked he found a way to answer by talking about Krishna. Sometimes he would call out Krishna's name and shiver with ecstasy. Some of them openly said he was crazy, others thought he might be ill. Looking for help, his students turned to Gangadas.

'Nimai Pandit no longer teaches us properly. How will we learn? Please speak to him and find out what is wrong.' Hearing this plea, Gangadas called for Nimai.

'I am glad you are now a Vaishnava, Nimai, but please don't stop teaching. It is your duty to help these students complete their studies. You can be a devotee of Krishna and still carry on your work.'

Nimai was respectful to his teacher, and took these words seriously. He said he would teach the whole town the true meaning of scripture in such a way that no one could find fault with his words. The next morning he sat down at the main entrance to the town of Navadvip and gathered his students round him, like stars surrounding the full moon. There he began to lecture. As he spoke, he proved conclusively, point by point, that Krishna is the essence of everything.

Many townsfolk came to hear him and listened in stunned silence. Some tried to argue with him, but none could contradict anything he said. As the day passed he talked on in deep ecstasy. The sun sank to the horizon and still his audience listened in rapt attention.

Late in the evening a brahmin happened by, chanting a verse of Sanskrit poetry describing the beauty of Krishna who wears a garland of forest flowers with a peacock feather in his hair. Nimai overheard this verse and lapsed into a trance. He trembled like a leaf and tears poured from his eyes as all looked on in wondering silence. Gadadhara, who was close beside him, silenced the brahmin and took Nimai in his arms. As everyone gathered round he gently brought Nimai round.

'What happened?' asked Nimai. His shocked students assured him all was well, and together they all went to the Ganges to bathe.

Early next morning Nimai was surprised to find his students assembled at his house carrying their books and patiently waiting for him to teach them. He bathed and dressed, then sat in their midst. They listened, full of concentration, as he taught them all through the day, explaining how all life depends upon Krishna and how Krishna is in everything.

'Krishna's power lives in all bodies as the breath of life,' he said. 'It is this that we love. When the body dies and Krishna leaves, even if it belongs to my father or mother, I love it no more and burn the body to ashes. Therefore, truly it is Krishna whom we all love, all of the time.'

He taught in a way they had never heard before, patiently convincing them of Krishna consciousness, putting forward sound and indisputable arguments for every point of philosophy, always reaching the conclusion that they devote themselves to Krishna, the Supreme Lord who is found in all of life and in every word of scripture. Six hours passed, and not a murmur came from any student. At last he concluded.

'As long as you have life in your body, serve Krishna's lotus feet.' He paused and looked closely at each of them.

'What have I been saying these last few days? I cannot remember.'

Hesitantly, they told him all that had occurred over the last ten days; how he had fallen repeatedly into trance; how he had bewildered them with his explanations; how he had defeated the whole town with his new philosophy of Krishna consciousness.

'Why didn't you stop me?' appealed Nimai. 'It was your duty to restrain me.'

'We were afraid to challenge you,' they answered. 'You spoke absolute truth which none could contradict.'

There seemed no more to say.

'I must leave you,' announced Nimai. 'You are free to go to whomever you like. I bless you all to be fearless, to go where your hearts lead you. From now on I can speak only of Krishna.' With this he tied up his bundle of books.

'Now we have heard you, how can we learn from anyone else?' His students wept. 'We will carry your words in our hearts.' Then they too tied up their books, as tearfully he embraced them one by one.

'All of you take shelter of Krishna and always chant his name.'

'But how shall we chant?' they wanted to know.

He taught them a prayer made of Krishna's names:

> *hari haraye namah krishna yadavaya namah*
> *gopala govinda rama sri madhusudana*

'I bow to Hari, to Krishna descendant of Yadu,
O Gopala, Govinda, Rama, O Madhusudana!'

Clapping his hands he started the chant, and they joined in. As the chant grew he became more absorbed, and the singing grew louder, bringing out the people to see what was happening. From all over Navadvip they flocked to see this wonder. Nimai, once the proud young pandit who paraded through the town, was transformed into Vishvambhar, the ecstatic and merciful devotee of Krishna who gave shelter to the people and led them in the glorious chanting of Krishna's names.

From now on, Navadvip would also be transformed.

EACH MORNING the Vaishnavas of Navadvip met at the riverbank. There they bathed in the holy Ganges and prayed together. To their delight, young Vishvambhar began to join them. He washed and dried their clothes, fetched sandal-wood and flowers for their worship, and made himself useful in any way he could. Later in the day he visited them in their homes, always bringing gifts. They hesitated to accept his service, but his wish was to care for the Vaishnavas, and they loved him for it. They knew that he was destined for great-ness: before long they would be serving him rather then he serving them. For the time being, though, they welcomed him as a new member of their community and accepted his offerings.

Seeing he was now one of them they told him of their fears of persecution. They were worried that they had enemies among the caste brahmins, who resented their independence and their different ways, and who would criticise them to the Muslim magistrate, Chand Kazi. The Vaishnavas favoured a religion based on love, in which anyone could pray directly to Krishna and receive God's grace without need for the brahmin's priestly ceremonies. They feared that the Kazi, urged on by the brahmins, would suppress them and even imprison their leaders. Vishvambhar listened to what they had to say and encouraged them.

'Who are these people that criticise you? Whoever they are you have no need to fear them. Krishna will always protect his devotees.'

He gave them his promise that he himself would protect them. Hearing this they believed they would be safe, so long as he was with them.

ONE DAY GADADHARA CAME to take his friend Nimai for a walk across the fields to Advaita's house. Advaita Acharya was the acknowledged elder among the Vaishnavas, the one they looked to for guidance. Gadadhara wanted him to see how Nimai had changed. He hoped Advaita would confirm what they all now believed, that Vishvambhar was destined to be their saviour.

For his part, Advaita had hoped for this opportunity. He had been watching Nimai from a distance ever since he first noticed him as the younger brother of Vishvarup. Secretly he had hoped that Nimai would be Krishna's answer to his prayers.

Advaita saw that Nimai had undergone a profound transformation into a thoughtful and spiritually absorbed young man. He was now unusually tall, and his commanding height added to his striking beauty. Along with this, his new modesty and calm assurance gave him a dignified and masterful air. When Advaita saw this effulgent figure approaching he felt himself in the presence of Krishna.

'You have come at last, my lord,' he said. 'We Vaishnavas have been waiting a long time. Please stay and always inspire us to chant Krishna's name.'

Advaita brought out the lamps and incense normally reserved for the worship of Vishnu, and with them he worshipped Vishvambhar. He finished by falling at his feet, reciting a mantra in praise of Krishna.

namo brahmanya devaya
go brahmana hitaya ca
jagad dhitaya krsnaya
govindaya namo namah

'I offer my respects to Krishna, lord of the brahmins,
benefactor of the cows, the brahmins and the whole
world. My repeated obeisances unto Govinda.'

Gadadhara saw that Advaita considered Vishvambhar as his
worshipful lord whom he was ready to serve; but he felt
embarrassed to see a respected elder of the community offer
such veneration to his intimate friend. Aware of Gadadhara's
discomfort, Advaita quietly advised the young man.

'You will soon understand that this friend of yours is no
ordinary person.'

Hearing these words and witnessing Advaita's change of
heart, Gadadhara silently vowed that from that day on he
would serve Vishvambhar as his personal master. The two
young friends Gadadhara and Vishvambhar returned home
and became inseparable. Vishvambhar's mother always
worried for her son's safety, and she made a special request
to Gadadhara.

'Please stay near us, dear boy, and always look after my son.'

Whenever his friend was lost in ecstasy Gadadhara
protected him, when he trembled with emotion Gadadhara
held him, and when Vishvambhar fainted while chanting
Krishna's name Gadadhara was there to catch him.

DAY AND NIGHT Vishvambhar called upon the name of Krishna and cried oceans of tears. Rumours spread of his transformation and attracted more attention to the Vaishnavas. The orthodox brahmins, who already regarded the Vaishnavas as sentimentalists who were undermining traditional religious authority, now openly opposed them. As the Vaishnavas had feared, some of the brahmins complained to the Muslim authorities. Word came that Chand Kazi was planning to arrest some of them. Shrivas in particular, as principle organiser, was afraid for himself and his family.

Vishvambhar heard of this and went to Shrivas's house. He found him worshipping Lord Narasingha, the lion-like form of Vishnu who protects his devotees from harm. Vishvambhar stood before Shrivas and roared like a lion. Shrivas had never seen Vishvambhar like this. He saw him transformed into Narasingha and trembled in fear.

'Don't you know yet who I am, Shrivas? I am the one you have always worshipped. I have heard your prayers and come to protect you.' Shrivas was stunned and at the same time filled with ecstasy. He prayed to Vishvambhar.

'O Lord, I did not recognise you. Disguised as an ordinary person you washed my clothes and served me, and so I was bewildered. Now I realise that you are Vishnu, you are Krishna, and you are Narasingha. My fear is gone.'

Vishvambhar told him to bring the rest of his family so they could also see him as Narasingha. Shrivas called his wife, children, and all his household to see this wonder. They brought the articles of worship from their household altar and used them to worship Vishvambhar. He accepted their worship and assured them that they need not be afraid. At any moment he could change the heart of the Kazi or the hearts of any of his subjects.

'In case you don't believe me, I will show you my powers,' said Vishvambhar. He looked into the eyes of Shrivas's four-year-old niece Narayani and commanded her.

'Chant Krishna's name, Narayani, and weep in ecstasy.'

The little girl started to sing Krishna's names, and as she did so she laughed and cried. From that day she was devoted to Vishvambhar—and Shrivas with all his household never feared the Kazi again.

Vishvambhar had now established devotion for Krishna as the theme of his life. He had Advaita as his mentor; he had his intimate friend Gadadhara; and his trusted helper Shrivas. Yet there remained one more close companion he must find before he was ready to embark upon his life's mission.

NITYANANDA WAS BORN in the village of Ekachakra, East Bengal. From childhood he had been adored by everyone. He led his friends in endless playful re-enacting of the lives of Krishna and Rama. This play so absorbed them day and night that they forgot even to go home to eat. One day when he was twelve years old a sannyasi stayed at his house. The holy man sat through the night speaking with his father about Krishna, and created a deep impression. In the morning when the sannyasi was ready to leave, he made a momentous request.

'Please give me your son as my travelling companion. He is a special child, and I will train him to be a great teacher.'

Nityananda's father and mother were shocked by this proposal, but they agreed to part with their beloved son, though he was their life and soul. Shortly afterwards his father died from a broken heart.

The boy followed his new master as he travelled from place to place, serving him and learning from him to practice yoga and recite the scriptures. When Nityananda reached manhood he took leave of his teacher and went on alone. For the next twenty years, filled with love for Krishna, he was on perpetual pilgrimage around the holy places of India. As he travelled, sometimes he laughed and sometimes he cried.

On his journeys Nityananda met the great mystic Madhavendra Puri, who was an ecstatic Vaishnava always absorbed in love for Radha and Krishna. The two embraced and spoke for a long time. While speaking they were frequently overcome with spiritual emotion to the point of tears. Nityananda recognised Madhavendra as his spiritual master, and became his disciple. Madhavendra had other disciples, among them Advaita Acharya and Isvara Puri, who was Vishvambhar's guru. In this way Nityananda became spiritually related to Vishvambhar and to the Vaishnavas of Navadvip.

Having found his guru and heard from him about Krishna, Nityananda went to Vrindavan, Krishna's home. There he stayed, awaiting divine guidance to show him his destiny. One day he heard that in Navadvip a great Vaishnava saint had arisen chanting the names of Krishna and inspiring the whole region. He knew he must meet this saint. So he made his way to Navadvip, where a brahmin gave him shelter in his house.

VISHVAMBHAR HAD AN UNUSUAL DREAM.

'I saw a majestic figure who reminded me of Krishna's brother Balarama,' he told his friends. 'He stood outside my house calling my name. I am sure someone special has arrived in Navadvip to see me. We must find him.'

His friends spent the morning looking for this special person, returning without success. Vishvambhar decided he must look himself, and in the afternoon led them straight to the door of a brahmin's house. Inside they beheld a handsome man dressed in white cloth with his hair drawn into a top-knot. He was in deep meditation, unaware of his visitors. They saw at once that he was a great soul and all bowed before him. Vishvambhar stood before him and waited.

Nityananda opened his eyes. Standing before him he saw the very person he had been seeking for so long. Stunned with the recognition, he was unable to speak. Prompted by Vishvambhar, one of the devotees recited a verse about Krishna. When he heard Krishna being described, Nityananda shuddered and rolled upon the floor in floods of tears. Vishvambhar raised him and the two embraced, floating in an ocean of love.

For a long time they held each other, crying with joy. Then Nityananda told of his endless pilgrimage; how wherever he went he saw only the holy place but never Krishna; how he had searched for Krishna all his life; and now he had found him in Vishvambhar. The devotees looked on in wonder. They thought they were seeing Rama and his brother Laksmana, or the brothers Krishna and Balarama. From that day Nityananda stayed as a guest in Shrivas's house, and became Vishvambhar's closest associate.

5

THE MISSION BEGINS

AT HOME WITH HER SON and daughter-in-law, Sachi saw many unusual things. Once, when Vishvambhar brought Nityananda home for lunch, she watched the two friends eating together and before her eyes they were transformed into five-year-old boys, looking just like the brothers Krishna and Balarama. Seeing this Sachi fainted and Vishvambhar ran to pick her up. He helped her to her room where she wept and trembled, overcome by what she had seen. This was how she first began to realise the divine identities of her son and Nityananda.

Each night the two met at Shrivas's house, journeying deep into the ocean of spiritual love, singing and dancing with the devotees. In these ecstatic dances Nityananda lost all inhibition and any sense of where he was or what he was doing, while the company experienced ever greater joy.

Day and night Vishvambhar danced amid the devotees at Shrivas's house. On some occasions he felt himself to be the Supreme Lord and displayed mystical powers accompanied by miraculous visions. When this happened the devotees became overwhelmed and speechless. Then his mood would change as he once more became a humble devotee, weeping and embracing his friends, begging them to show him Krishna.

ONE HOT DAY after dancing and singing together for a long time, they were all exhausted. Vishvambhar planted a mango seed in the dry earth. Before everyone's eyes it grew into a tree and bore ripe mangoes. Vishvambhar collected about two hundred fruits, each of them juicy and without a seed, and fed them to all present. The tree lived on to produce fruits daily throughout the year.

MURARI GUPTA CAME to see Vishvambhar. As an old friend he showed his respects first to Vishvambhar, then to Nityananda who sat beside him. Vishvambhar told him to go home.

'I will teach you something,' he said.

Murari went home and slept. In his dream he saw Nityananda walking in front of Vishvambhar. He saw Nityananda change into Balarama, carrying a plough and club, and he saw Vishvambhar as Krishna with a peacock feather in his hair. When he awoke he remembered what

Vishvambhar had said earlier and believed the dream had shown him that Nityananda was Balarama, Krishna's elder brother, and Vishvambhar was Krishna. Balarama always protected Krishna and was therefore honoured first. Murari returned to Vishvambhar and this time offered his respects first to Nityananda then to Vishvambhar.

'Now you have understood,' said Vishvambhar, pleased with his friend. 'Anyone who wishes to be my devotee should first venerate Nityananda. If they do that they will be dear to me.'

Vishvambhar had special love for Murari and later revealed to him that in a previous birth he had been Hanuman, servant of Rama.

Another devotee who came regularly to Shrivas's house was Suklambara, a simple soul who lived in Navadvip and was loved by all the Vaishnavas. He devoted his time to chanting Krishna's names. He kept body and soul together by begging alms from nearby houses, collecting broken rice in a small bag. Broken rice was the poorest quality of rice, but was his only food. One day Vishvambhar seized a handful of this rice and ate it, exactly as Krishna had once eaten the rice brought to him in Dvaraka by his childhood friend Sudama. Vishvambhar chewed the morsels of rice with relish. When Suklambara protested that such broken rice was not fit for him to eat, Vishvambhar laughed. Then he taught everyone present.

'Chanting Krishna's names is all you need for success in this age. The name is the incarnation of Krishna. When you chant Krishna's name you are directly in his presence. No other method—either study or penance or good works—is necessary for salvation. Be like Suklambara, patient and humble, like the tree that neither protests nor asks favours. Simply accept whatever comes as the grace of God. In this mood you will be able to chant Krishna's names constantly.'

Vishvambhar decided the time had come to bring Advaita Acharya closer. Since their previous encounter Advaita had moved away from Navadvip to his house in Shantipur, some twenty miles away, where he awaited Vishvambhar's call to join him. Now his lord wanted to include him in the mystic assemblies each night at Shrivas's house, so he sent word for him to come. Advaita had so far witnessed Vishvambhar in the role of a devotee, but Vishvambhar knew that what Advaita wanted was to see his divine majesty. Consequently, on the day Advaita was to come, a transformation took place among Vishvambhar and his companions.

When Advaita arrived at Shrivas's house, he found Vishvambhar sitting on a throne in the midst of his devotees. Nityananda held an umbrella over his head, Gadadhara served him on one side and Shrivas on the other. Advaita saw the scene transformed into a heavenly vision, with the chief demigods such as Brahma and Shiva also present, worshipping Vishvambhar as their master. In ecstasy Advaita, along with his wife Sita, fell at the feet of Vishvambhar, who placed those divine feet on Advaita's head. Advaita's dream was fulfilled and he was beside himself with joy. At that moment he surrendered himself fully to the service of Vishvambhar.

'I have come to teach everyone to be loving servants of Krishna,' said Vishvambhar. 'In every town and village I will spread my movement of love for God.'

Hearing these words, Advaita added his own special request.

'Please, Lord, when you preach, do not forget the less fortunate souls—the poor, the downtrodden, the fallen and the foolish. Include them all in your mercy.'

'It doesn't matter who they are, they shall be included,' replied Vishvambhar. 'Only those who are too proud will escape. Even though they pretend to be religious, if they are proud I cannot help them.'

The nightly chanting sessions continued, now including Advaita, and the numbers grew. Vishvambhar embraced each newcomer as an old friend. As he welcomed them, each saw in him the divine person they were looking for; some saw the magnificent Vishnu, some lordly Rama, and some the all-attractive Krishna. At the same time they saw in him a humble servant of Krishna, who prayed and wept in the mood of a devotee.

Sachi also came and watched her son carried away by ecstasies, hair and clothing in disarray, falling to the ground and rolling in the dust. She feared he would hurt himself, but since she could not prevent him she prayed to Krishna that he would not be harmed, and that she would always be absorbed with him in singing Krishna's names.

DURING THEIR ALL-NIGHT CHANTING at Shrivas's house, they felt time stand still, as if in a single night they passed an eternity. Sometimes the chanters caught a glimpse of Vishvambhar's immensity, when for a few moments he showed his magnificence. Usually he was wrapped in his mood of devotion, in love with Krishna. However there was one occasion when without reservation he showed his divine nature.

On this day he stood to dance as usual, then turned toward the altar in Shrivas's shrine room and sat down there in the place meant for Vishnu. Before everyone's eyes he was transformed into a dazzling divine personality. All present could understand they were in the presence of Vishnu himself. They felt the shadows of illusion fall away and saw Vishvambhar for the first time as he truly was, as the Supreme Lord of all. So began what they later called the Great Revelation, a mystical transformation that lasted for twenty-one hours.

In awe they worshipped the Divine Person before them. They began by bathing Vishvambhar with pots of Ganges water scented with herbs and oils. Nityananda was first to bathe Vishvambhar's head, then each took their turn, including the servants and children. Everyone had the chance to offer homage and taste the flavour of eternal devotional service.

After bathing Vishvambhar they dressed him in fresh garments and massaged his feet with fragrant oils. They brought him offerings of fruits and flowers, and performed the arati ceremony to Vishnu. Next they wanted to feed him. Running here and there, they gathered the best foods from wherever they could, searching all over town to collect fruits, sweets and dairy products to prepare wonderful dishes for their Lord.

As Vishvambhar sat and ate he recalled the lives of some of those present, speaking of private occasions known only to each of them.

He reminded Shrivas of the time he had listened to a talk on the *Srimad Bhagavatam* and been overwhelmed to hear about Krishna. Shrivas had broken down weeping, while his fellow students, not understanding what was wrong, had carried him outside and left him lying on the ground; Shrivas, hurt and misunderstood, had gone home to read the *Bhagavatam* again and again, his eyes brimming with tears.

'I saw your unhappiness and entered your heart, filling you with spiritual love,' he told Shrivas. 'That is why you always feel such bliss when you hear the *Bhagavatam*.'

He turned to Gangadas, his former teacher.

'Do you remember when, afraid of persecution by the Kazi, you set out at night with your family to cross the Ganges and escape from his soldiers? You could not find a boat, and as dawn approached you all stood on the bank shaking with fear. You were on the point of throwing yourselves into the river when I came as a ferryman to rescue you. It was I who saved you, Gangadas, I who carried you and your family across the Ganges.' When he heard this, Gangadas fainted.

Vishvambhar remembered his old friend Shridhar the banana seller, whom he used to provoke so mischievously in his youth. He spoke to those nearby.

'Go down to the bank of the Ganges and listen for someone calling upon the name of Krishna. Bring that person to me.'

Some of them went in the direction of the Ganges and there they heard a voice in the darkness. It was Shridhar. At the end of each day, having sold his bananas in the market, Shridhar spent the night in prayer, repeating Krishna's name beside the flowing waters. They brought him to the house and into the midst of the gathering. Blinking, Shridhar came face to face with the same Nimai who used to joke with him at his banana stall. Seeing Nimai transformed into a divine being, Shridhar almost fainted.

'Shridhar, you always call my name, so now I have called your name and brought you here. You served me well, giving me everything I asked even without being paid, and you let me trick you many times. Now I want to give you any boon you care to ask. But first I give you the eyes to see me as I am.'

Before his eyes Shridhar saw Vishvambhar transformed into Krishna playing his flute.

'Come, if you wish you can have a whole planet—just ask.'

Shridhar fixed his eyes on Krishna's feet.

'Just be my master. That is all I want. And to sing your name.'

'Then I bless you with pure devotional service. That is the greatest gift I can give.'

Shridhar wept with joy and everyone sang Krishna's names.

Vishvambhar was specially fond of Haridas, who had borne great suffering for the sake of his devotion to Krishna. He was raised a Muslim but at an early age found faith in Krishna and a deep attachment to chanting Krishna's names. Long ago he had been brought before the king for punishment. Haridas fearlessly told the king that the Qur'an and the Puranas both describe the same God.

'All the people of the world worship the same God according to their natures and the scriptures God has given them,' he said.

But the king was hard-hearted. He had Haridas beaten in twenty-two market places, then thrown in the Ganges and left for dead. His lifeless body was carried downstream. Miraculously he was washed ashore and recovered. Later he was taken in and befriended by Advaita Acharya. All this had happened before Vishvambhar was born. Haridas had prayed with Advaita, and together they had implored the Supreme Lord to descend into this world and rescue people from their ignorance and suffering.

'My heart broke when you were beaten. You felt no anger against your attackers and on account of your love I could not harm them. I myself took the blows from your back so that you felt no pain. I am your servant, Haridas. For your sake I am here. I will do anything for you.'

Haridas prayed to Vishvambhar that he would always be able to serve the Vaishnavas, and Vishvambhar blessed him to forever love and serve Krishna and his devotees. Haridas's ceaseless chanting of Krishna's names made him the example for all Vaishnavas to follow.

'What of Mukunda' asked Shrivas, 'what benediction will you give him?' But Vishvambhar had no blessing for Mukunda.

Mukunda had a beautiful voice and Vishvambhar had always loved to hear him sing. They had been together since Mukunda enrolled as one of the first pupils in Nimai's Sanskrit academy. However, he became unhappy with Mukunda because he mixed with teachers opposed to devotional service to Krishna. As a consequence of this, Vishvambhar had barred him from their gatherings. Mukunda however was unable to stay away; that very night he was in the room, hidden behind a curtain.

Hearing from his hiding place that Vishvambhar had nothing for him, the distraught Mukunda whispered to Shrivas, asking if he would ever be allowed to see Vishvambhar again? Shrivas went to Vishvambhar and made a plea on Mukunda's behalf.

'After ten million births he will see me,' responded Vishvambhar, 'This is certain.'

'I will, I will!' came Mukunda's involuntary cry from behind the curtain. Vishvambhar, laughing, called him out. Weeping with relief and happiness he was brought before his master.

'My blessing to you is that I will spread my love through your voice. Wherever I am you will be there as my singer, and when my devotees hear your voice their hearts will melt.'

'Haribol, Haribol!' cried the devotees, and Mukunda once more was able to sing for Vishvambhar.

EACH EVENING AT SHRIVAS'S HOUSE when they began singing, Vishvambhar had the doors closed so that only his devotees were allowed in, for some were ready to disapprove of what they were doing and might try to disrupt the meetings. On one occasion Shrivas made an exception and allowed a monk to secretly watch the chanting. Vishvambhar danced and sang as usual, but after some time he stopped.

'Why do I feel no ecstasy?' he asked. 'An intruder is hiding here. Who is it?'

'It is a pure-hearted monk whom I secretly allowed in,' admitted Shrivas.

Vishvambhar sent the monk away. He left without complaint, simply thinking himself fortunate to have had a glimpse of Vishvambhar's dancing. Understanding his heart, Vishvambhar relented and called him back to openly join in.

Despite their caution, rumours circulated about what went on behind their closed doors. One night someone left a flagon of wine outside their entrance in view of passers-by, so as to make it look as if riotous celebrations were going on inside.

Rumours began to spread. Some said Shrivas was permitting illicit practices and that he would ruin the reputation of the neighbourhood. The influential brahmins of Navadvip started speaking against him, fearing his gatherings would attract unwanted attention from their Muslim rulers, and jeopardise the brahmin's power and influence. As it turned out, word had already reached the Muslim king that a religious revival was stirring in Navadvip, and questions were being asked.

VISHVAMBHAR'S FIRM INTENTION was to start a popular movement based on communal chanting of God's names. He sent out his two most experienced and trusted companions, Nityananda and Haridas, to invite people to chant the name of Krishna. Each day the two of them went from house to house with a simple request.

'Please chant Krishna's name, worship Krishna and teach others about Krishna.'

Most people were happy to hear this message, but some resented its direct and uncompromising appeal. Still Nityananda and Haridas continued, undeterred by any opposition they encountered.

One day they came upon two drunkards brawling in the street. These were the notorious brothers Jagai and Madhai. Despite being raised in a good family they had become extortionists and murderers who terrorised the people of

Navadvip. Passers-by warned Nityananda not to interfere with these dangerous men, who were feared even by officers of the law. But their warnings only encouraged Nityananda. He thought it would be glorious if this wretched pair could be rescued from their degraded condition, then everyone would give credit to Vishvambhar. Ignoring the warnings, Niyananda fearlessly approached them.

'Krishna is your father,' he called loudly. 'Chant Krishna's name, give up your sins and worship Krishna!'

Stupefied by drink, Jagai and Madhai looked in surprise to see who dared confront them. They saw two Vaishnavas, people who represented everything they detested. Filled with rage they leapt at them, intent on doing grievous harm. Nityananda and Haridas ran for their lives, pursued by the drunken pair.

'Thanks to you we could get ourselves killed,' shouted Haridas, but Nityananda laughed. The drunkards were confused and could not catch the nimble devotees; all they could do was yell threats and foul language. Nityananda and Haridas safely reached Shrivas's house and breathlessly told their master what had happened. Vishvambhar was pleased to hear of their bold attempt and congratulated them.

Haridas, however, was worried that his partner would try again and endanger them all, so he told Advaita Acharya about Nityananda's wild ways and asked him to talk sense to him. All Advaita did was assure Haridas that very soon he would see those two ruffians miraculously transformed. Hearing this, Haridas resigned himself to whatever might follow.

Jagai and Madhai continued their drunken ways. They started wandering close to Shrivas's house at night, drawn by the sound of singing and musical instruments coming from within. In their inebriated state they would dance to the music and join in the singing, unaware of its spiritual potency. Sometimes they saw Vishvambhar pass by and shouted after him.

'Nimai Pandit, we like your music! We'll visit you and bring you gifts.'

Vishvambhar took no notice, but one evening Nityananda met them again in the street. They recognised him and demanded to know his name. In reply he only joked with them. This made Madhai furious and without warning he attacked Nityananda, striking him a severe blow on his forehead with a broken pot. Nityananda was badly cut and his blood began to flow. At this Jagai was remorseful, because even he feared the consequences of harming a holy man like Nityananda. He caught hold of his brother to restrain him and the two were locked in a struggle. Nityananda, although his forehead was bleeding, was unafraid. He stood his ground, filled with determination to rescue these two offenders.

All of sudden Vishvambhar appeared with miraculous speed. He saw Nityananda wounded and bleeding, his assailants before him. Filled with anger, Vishvambhar drew himself up to his full height and summoned Vishnu's divine weapon, the disk that severs the heads of demons. In defence of Nityananda he was ready to use it. The two brothers saw him towering above them like death personified, the blazing disk spinning on his outstetched hand. They were paralysed with fear. At that moment Nityananda intervened.

'Do not kill them. These two are mine and I want them spared. Give them to me. Though Madhai attacked me, his brother Jagai tried to stop him.' When Vishvambhar heard that Jagai had tried to hold back his brother, he softened toward him.

'You tried to protect my Nityananda, so from this day I give you pure love for Krishna.'

With these words Vishvambhar embraced Jagai, who collapsed to the ground in tears. Jagai and Madhai's hearts beat as one, for they did everything together. No sooner had Jagai's heart changed than Madhai's also changed and he too fell at Vishvambhar's feet begging for mercy.

'You injured the body of my beloved Nityananda, so I cannot save you,' said Vishvambhar to Madhai. 'Only if you fall down before him and hold on to his feet can you be saved.' Madhai fell at Nityananda's feet and begged his forgiveness. Nityananda had no need to forgive him, since he had not taken offence in the first place. He turned to Vishvambhar.

'Lord, you have the power to show your mercy to Madhai. Whatever good deeds I have done I give them to him. Now you please save him.'

'Then you must embrace him,' said Vishvambhar. 'He will be saved by your touch.' Nityananda took Madhai in his arms and embraced him. As he did so Madhai was infused with pure love. The two brothers, by now completely subdued, prayed before Vishvambhar and surrendered themselves to him.

'Sin no more,' he said. 'Your sins are washed away.' Then he ordered his companions, 'Bring them to our assembly tonight. I will chant with these two lost souls and make them the best of devotees.'

That evening the kirtan was more intense than usual. Before long, Jagai and Madhai were dancing with the devotees and their bodies were touching Vishvambhar. They underwent a profound transformation. Tears began pouring from their eyes, their bodies shivered and their hairs stood on end. Falling to the ground they rolled on the floor. Coming to their knees and finding their voices they glorified their saviours with eloquent words from deep within.

'You are the Supreme Lord,' they said to Nityananda, 'yet we tried to hurt you and we made your body bleed. Still you show us your mercy and forgiveness.'

'You are Vishnu himself,' they prayed to Vishvambhar. 'Descended into this world to forgive all sinners. Now you have saved us.'

As the two brothers wept uncontrollably, Vishvambhar asked his devotees to bless them. The brothers fell before each one present and received their blessings.

'Rise Jagai and Madhai, you are now my servants. By Nityananda's mercy you are purified.' As he spoke these words, Vishvambhar's body turned black. 'This blackness comes from their sins,' he exclaimed, and while he danced the blackness faded until his body shone bright and fair.

'They are no longer sinners,' he declared. 'I have burned away their sins. Now Jagai and Madhai belong to me and I personally live in their bodies. Whoever serves them serves me.' So saying he gave them his own flower garlands.

Seeing the profound transformation in these two abominable sinners, the devotees knew that they were seeing the greatest miracle of all, the proof of Vishvambhar's love. Here was a sign of things to come, of the flood of love for God that would engulf all who came in touch with him—and Vishvambhar said it was all due to Nityananda's mercy.

WANDERING CAREFREE in the streets of Navadvip, Nityananda came face to face with Madhai. Falling at his feet, Madhai washed them with his tears.

'Please forgive this ungrateful soul for the harm I caused you,' he prayed.

'Rise Madhai, you are mine and I am yours,' said Nityananda. 'Does a father take offence from his infant son? You have received my master's mercy, therefore there is no fault in you.'

'Lord, one thing troubles me. I grievously hurt countless people of Navadvip. I don't even know who they are so I can't beg their forgiveness. How can I make amends?'

'Build a bathing ghat beside the Ganges,' Nityananda instructed him, 'Greet all who come to bathe in her sacred waters, and humbly beg their forgiveness.'

So Madhai, his heart heavy with remorse, levelled a platform beside the Ganges and dug steps to serve as a bathing place. There he stayed, spade in hand to maintain the place, every day from dawn to dusk. Chanting the names of Krishna, he served all who came to bathe, and cared for their clothes.

'Forgive whatever offences I have made against you,' he begged each one with folded hands. 'Please show your mercy to this fallen soul.'

When the townspeople saw this change in Madhai and his brother Jagai, they were astounded.

'Nimai Pandit is no ordinary person,' they said. 'Truly he has divine power to change the hearts of two such as these.' From that day none of the townspeople of Navadvip spoke ill of Vishvambhar, the saviour of Jagai and Madhai.

NEWS OF THE NIGHTLY GATHERINGS at Shrivas's house spread among the people of Navadvipa. They wanted to witness them, but knew their Muslim overlords would not permit kirtan to be held openly. If only Vishvambhar would come out among the people and let everyone hear for themselves the chanting that had so miraculously transformed the hearts of Jagai and Madhai.

More and more homes were heeding the requests by Vishvambhar's loyal preachers, and the sound of drums and cymbals could be heard in the evenings coming from houses across the town. Daily, visitors brought Vishvambhar gifts. He bade them faithfully to sing Krishna's names, and taught them the *maha-mantra*, the great chant for deliverance:

> *Hare Krishna Hare Krishna*
> *Krishna Krishna Hare Hare*
> *Hare Rama Hare Rama*
> *Rama Rama Hare Hare*

He told them to chant these names at any time or place, either as *japa*, praying softly to themselves, or as sankirtan, singing together with their family and friends. And so it began.

Each day at sunset people gathered in their homes to sing, and melodious chanting began to spread from village to village throughout the district. Unease also spread as some muttered disapproval and complained to their Muslim rulers. Matters came to a head one day when Chand Kazi walked through the town and heard the sound of sankirtan coming from all directions. He sent armed guards into several homes, including Shrivas's house. They seized the clay drums and broke them, arrested some of the chanters and beat them, while others fled.

'From now on *sankirtan* is banned,' ordered the Kazi. 'Today I am excusing you, but if I find anyone doing this in future I will seize their property and forcibly convert them into Muslims.'

Shocked and afraid, devotees hurried to Vishvambhar with the news. He was defiant.

'Carry on with your sankirtan and do not fear. I will protect you.' Despite hearing these encouraging words from Vishvambhar, the people were still afraid of the Kazi. Yet they continued with their chanting, and by so doing they called down Krishna's mercy.

IT WAS TIME FOR PUBLIC ACTION. Vishvambhar sent out word calling all the townspeople to gather for a huge demonstration in the form of a sankirtan procession that very evening. He wanted a great festival, and told them to decorate the roads and organise themselves in each of the nine districts of Navadvip.

'Bring torches from every home. Bring musical instruments. We will have sankirtan—let the Kazi try to stop us!'

The townships buzzed with excitement. At last they were to witness Vishvambhar's ecstatic dancing. For one whole year they had waited, hearing only rumours of events in Shrivas's house, while their eagerness to join his movement had grown to a deep longing. Men busied themselves preparing torches and gathering musical instruments, and women decorated their homes with lamps and waterpots, coconuts and banana trees, and created artistic patterns on the ground outside the threshold of each house. As evening approached, Vishvambhar formed three *sankirtan* groups; one group led by Haridas;

a second by Advaita and Shrivas; and a third by Vishvambhar with Nityananda and Gadadhara dancing either side of him. Thus for the first time Vishvambhar came out to perform his chanting and dancing in public for all to witness.

As the setting sun tinged the sky with pink rays, the three groups set out from Shrivas's house, passing through each of the quarters of Navadvip. Vishvambhar danced along the shore of the Ganges, past his childhood playground where he first met Laksmidevi, past the place where as Nimai Pandit he had taught his students, past Madhai's ghat, through the gates of the town where he had discoursed into the night, all the while moving steadily toward the Kazi's palace. Around him crowded a huge and highly charged procession, everyone seeking a glimpse of their inspiring leader.

Beautiful Vishvambhar, his golden features shining, danced in their midst. His tall frame swayed with arms extended like golden pillars to the sky. His strong shoulders and broad chest were encircled with a garland of jasmine flowers reaching to his knees. His dark curling hair decorated with flowers framed his moonlike face, and tears rolled like pearls down his glowing cheeks. As he danced he sang the names of Krishna in pure joy while his body trembled, fragile as a kadamba flower caught in the wind. Watching him, the chanters floated in bliss. None could take their eyes from his glorious form.

Lit by thousands of torches, the night sky reverberated with the sound of massed drums and cymbals as a flood of maddened devotees converged upon the Kazi's home, surging through his grounds, trampling his flower gardens and setting light to his outer buildings. His guards fled without resistance and left the Kazi undefended. Fearing for his life he hid in his private quarters. Vishvambhar saw the wild state of the crowd and calmed them. Entering the inner courtyard, he sent a respected citizen inside to persuade Chand Kazi to come out, while he sat down outside his door and waited for him to appear. The Muslim ruler eventually emerged, shaking with fear. Vishvambhar assured him he was safe and respectfully offered him a seat.

IT HAPPENED THAT VISHVAMBHAR'S grandfather-in-law, Nilambara Cakravarti, had been like an uncle to Chand Kazi when he was young. Vishvambhar recalled this relationship by referring to the governor as uncle, and again promised no harm would befall him. The governor composed himself and exchanged words with Vishvambhar. For some time they discussed the relative merits of Hindu and Muslim scriptures. Then Vishvambhar put a question to him.

'Lately you have not interfered with us, even when we have chanted openly. And tonight we have brought our drums and cymbals right to your doorstep without hindrance. Why have you not tried to stop us?'

'I have been afraid,' admitted the Kazi. 'The night I ordered your drums to be broken I dreamt a terrifying lion-headed creature sprang upon my chest and threatened me. See the marks of his claws.'

He opened his shirt and showed the marks of a lion's claws on his chest. 'He demanded I stop persecuting you for chanting the names of Krishna and Hari, or he would kill me. The next day several of my men told me that when they came near your devotees to stop them from chanting, they felt flames scorch their faces and singe their beards. These things frightened me, so I decided to leave you be.' With tears in his eyes, the Kazi lowered his voice. 'In my heart I feel you to be the divine Vishnu whom the Hindus worship.'

'You have spoken the names of Krishna, Hari and Vishnu,' said Vishvambhar. 'Therefore you are now freed from all sins.' When he heard this Chand Kazi bent down and touched Vishvambhar's feet, begging his mercy. Then he stood up and spoke in a loud voice.

'From this day forward no descendant of mine shall hinder the sankirtan movement. This is my order.' He safely re-entered his home and everyone cheered, 'Hari! Hari!'

Vishvambhar led them again in chanting the holy names, and the crowds after much jubilation went peacefully to their beds. All those citizens of Navadvip who witnessed these events and saw Vishvambhar's ecstatic dancing on this night felt their lives were blessed forever.

6

FAREWELL TO FAMILY

AFTER THE KAZI'S PROCLAMATION, Vishvambhar and his company of Vaishnava friends were daily seen on the streets of Navadvip and neighbouring towns. They included singers, dancers and musicians with drums and cymbals. Their processions captured the hearts of the people and many became Vaishnavas.

A devotee composed a song in praise of their *sankirtan*.

When the sun arose in the east
The Golden Lord went out,
Through the towns and villages
With singers all about.

'Tathai, tathai,' called the drum
The cymbals chimed in time.
His ankle-bells shimmered, his golden form
Trembled with love divine.

'Mukunda, Madhava, Yadava, Hari!'
Filled every chanter's mouth.
They woke the people from their dream
With urgent words of truth

'For human life do you not care,
This gift so precious and high?
Why not serve Yasoda's son
As days and years drift by?'

'Each time the sun appears and sets,
Another day is gone.
Why stay idle, when you can please
The Lord of everyone?'

'Life is short and quickly passed,
Filled with sorrow and pain.
Leave aside your hopes and fears
And sing the holy name.'

'Taste the sweetness of Krishna's name,
Which rises like the sun.
It fills the world with purest light
And blesses everyone.'

—so sings Bhaktivinoda

AT SRIVAS'S HOUSE ONE NIGHT, soon after the great public procession, Vishvambhar was absorbed in singing with his associates. Shrivas's young son had been unwell and was being cared for in another room, when cries were heard. Shrivas went to see the cause and found his son had unexpectedly breathed his last and his family were calling out in deep distress. He begged them to restrain their cries lest they disturb Vishvambhar's chanting. Without informing his guests, he stayed quietly with his grieving family to comfort them. He reassured his wife that this was a blessed way for their child's soul to leave this world, in the presence of Vishvambhar and so many exalted souls, while hearing the singing of the names of the Lord.

'Our son has achieved life's greatest goal,' he said. 'He has passed away hearing Krishna's name. He is certainly liberated from birth and death and even now is in the spiritual world.' He appealed to his family to hold their grief in their hearts and not show their emotions until after Vishvambhar and the devotees had left. His words restrained them, and in silence they prepared the child's body for his last rites.

Saying nothing of his bereavement, Shrivas returned to the chanting where, thinking of the Lord's mercy, he chanted with even greater feeling than usual. After some time Vishvambhar stopped the kirtan.

'Shrivas, I am feeling unhappy. What sorrow has entered this house?'

'In your presence, Lord, there can be no sorrow,' answered Shrivas.

Vishvambhar was not convinced. He soon learned what had happened and became very grave. He realised Shrivas had not wanted to disturb him with the news. Thinking how much his devoted friends loved him, and how for his sake they would not openly grieve even for their own child, he wondered how he would ever be able to leave the company of those who loved him so dearly. He began to weep. Those near him heard him talk of leaving, but none knew what this could mean. Vishvambhar stirred himself and went to see the boy. With the household gathered round, he took the dead boy's hand in his and spoke to him gently.

'Why did you leave your father's house?'

The boy opened his eyes and spoke.

'Who is father and who is son? My karma brought me to this body and now it is time for me to leave and enter another body. You, Lord, control my destiny and I move according to your will, with no power to resist. My stay in Shrivas's home has been my great fortune. I beg forgiveness for my offences at his feet. Now, dear Lord of my heart, allow me to leave and bless me that I may never forget you.'

All heard the boy speak and watched in amazement as he fell silent, his body lifeless once more. Hearing these words of truth, Shrivas and his family were enlightened and their grief was washed away. Overcome, they touched Vishvambhar's feet and drowned their sorrows in tears of love.

Vishvambhar personally carried the child's body to the

Ganges, followed by Shrivas and his brothers. There they performed the last rites and burned the body to ashes. With chants of 'Hari!' they scattered those ashes into the ever-flowing waters of Mother Ganges, who has borne the tears and laughter of all who live upon her banks since time immemorial. Then Vishvambhar made a promise to Shrivas.

'Dear Shrivas, you have lost your earthly son, but because of your loving care for me and my brother Nityananda we are bound to you eternally as your spiritual sons.'

A MAID WORKED in Shrivas's house whose name was Duhkhi, which means sad. She laboured hard to keep the house clean and serve the family. While working each night she witnessed Vishvambhar's chanting. She was present during his Great Revelation, when she had the chance to offer service to him along with the family.

Every evening Duhkhi collected water from the Ganges, carrying many waterpots on her head. While coming and going she caught glimpses of Vishvambhar's secret dancing. Back and forth she toiled until a row of waterpots stood as evidence of her labours, ready for the devotees to refresh themselves. One night, Vishvambhar considered the waterpots standing there, each filled to the brim with Ganges water, and asked Shrivas who it was that worked so hard to fill them. Shrivas told him it was his servant Duhkhi.

'Duhkhi is not the name for such a faithful servant. In my heart she will always be Sukhi,' he declared. Sukhi means happy. From that night everyone called her by her new name, and Shrivas never again thought of her as his servant.

AS THE DAYS PASSED, Vishvambhar wandered from one ecstatic mood to another. Sometimes he felt the mood of Rama, sometimes Krishna, sometimes Narasingha. Each of the great avatars of Vishnu was revealed in him at different times. Sometimes, thinking himself Balarama, he laughed and danced wildly, calling for honey and wine. At such times only Nityananda could restrain him.

Increasingly he dwelt on his love for Krishna. He became absorbed in the emotions of the gopis, the girls who loved Krishna in the forests of Vrindavan, who joined Him in the mystical circle of his *rasa* dance. Their love for Krishna was the supreme expression of self-surrender. When Krishna left Vrindavan, the pain of separation felt by the gopis was almost unbearable. Now Vishvambhar's heart was filled with this same undying love. Like them he looked everywhere for Krishna but could not find Him. Overwhelmed by intense feelings of Krishna's absence he wept pitifully in the company of his friends. His mother could not bear to see him like this, so she stayed at home and simply cried for her son.

A young brahmin, a former student of Vishvambhar, heard about his ecstasies and was curious. People said Nimai Pandit had become a great saint, and he wanted to see for himself. So one day he crept into Vishvambhar's house to spy on him. He found him seated alone calling in distress the names 'Gopi' and 'Vrindavan.' To the student, previously versed in conventional worship, this behaviour was incomprehensible. He interrupted Vishvambhara's deep absorption and advised him not to call the word 'Gopi' and instead chant Krishna's names. Vishvambhar was in trance, feeling himself as a village girl in love with Krishna. Unaware who addressed him, he cried out.

'Krishna is a thief, what will I gain by chanting his name? Why should I worship Krishna, who went away to become a prince in Mathura and left us behind in Vrindavan?'

Saying this he seized a stick and chased away the young brahmin, who escaped unharmed only because some of Vishvambhar's friends intervened to save him. Shaken, the young man complained among his associates, who were sons of brahmins and accustomed to receiving honour from all. When they heard their fellow brahmin's story they grew indignant. This Nimai Pandit who they used to respect, they told one another, was losing his balance of mind and leading others astray. So they spread gossip against him and his followers, sowing seeds of envy and doubt among their community.

Vishvambhar heard what was happening and became thoughtful. He could not allow his fledgling sankirtan movement to be threatened by lies and gossip. He decided the time had come for him to enter the next stage of his life's mission, so in a quiet place he spoke to Nityananda.

'Dear Nitai, I came to this world to save people from pain and illusion. But if they mock me everything will be spoiled and they will have to continue suffering. Therefore I have decided to become a sannyasi. If I give up my family and beg at the doors of people's homes, they will respect me as a renunciant, and so they will be saved.' Nityananda listened to this proposal in silence.

'Please give me your permission,' Vishvambhar pleaded. 'If you want to see the world delivered, you must allow me to do this.'

'I have no power to prevent you,' replied Nityananda. 'You will do whatever you decide to do, and I trust that it will turn out to be right. But grant me one thing before you take this step: tell the others your intentions and hear what they have to say.'

Following this advice, Vishvambhar first spoke with Mukunda, whose singing he loved to hear. From childhood they had known each other and Mukunda's gentle nature had always made him a source of good advice. Mukunda was happy to see Vishvambhar. At his request he sang him a beautiful song about Krishna. Then Vishvambhar spoke of his intentions.

'I will shave my hair, Mukunda, do not doubt me. I will do this and travel the world as a sannyasi.'

Mukunda was distraught. He knew Vishvambhar could not be dissuaded. With heavy heart he made one request.

'Please stay with us a little longer so we can sing together a few more times, then do whatever you must.'

Next Vishvambhar spoke with Gadadhara. Their love for each other was tender, for Gadadhara cared for him and his mother like a second brother. When Gadadhara heard the news he felt deeply distressed.

'Why all of a sudden must you leave household life? By shaving his head did anyone ever attain Krishna? And what will become of your dear mother? Without you she will be all alone and will not be able to live. You will kill her! Just stay here and live as a householder, and together we will serve Krishna. But if you are determined, then do as you please.'

As Vishvambhar's intentions became known everyone was upset. Seeing their misery he felt great unhappiness.

'I promise you whatever happens we will never be separated,' he told his friends. 'You are all my eternal associates. In life after life you will see me. Whenever I come to this world you will be with me, and you can always find me in the bliss of sankirtan and by worshipping my deity form in your homes.' With these words he calmed their fears.

Last of all he had to tell his mother. When she learned that her son would leave her she could hardly stay alive. Weary with weeping, she poured out her heart to him.

'O Nimai, please don't go. How will I live without seeing your moonlike face, your lotus eyes and long arms. You fill my house with light even without lamps. Your followers and friends are here—stay with them and have your sankirtan here in our house. Nitai will help you. If you abandon your mother, how will you then teach religion and love of God?'

At first Vishvambhar said nothing. Then he spoke softly to give her courage.

'Listen mother dear, hear my secret. For many lifetimes you have been my mother. When I appeared as Vamana you were my mother Aditi; as Devahuti you bore me as Kapila; you were Kaushalya and I your son Ramachandra; then you became Devaki and I was born as your son Krishna. You are my mother birth after birth and we can never be separated. This is the truth.' Hearing her son speak these words Saci was consoled and regained her life.

Having given notice of his intentions, Vishvambhar abided by Mukunda's request and let matters rest for a while. He entered a last exuberant phase in sharing love with his dear friends and followers in Navadvipa. In the back of their minds they all knew he would soon be leaving them, so they immersed themselves more than ever in tasting the happiness that only Vishvambhar's presence could bring. In these final days the kirtans were sweeter, the glances more laden with love, the exchanges deeper, since all knew that these may be the last of their kind.

THE WINTER'S DAY of Makara-Sankranti dawned, the day the sun moves into Capricorn. Vishvambhar whispered to Nityananda.

'Tonight I will leave. I will go to Katwa where a pure-hearted monk, Kesava Bharati, is staying. From him I will accept the order of sannyasa. Only five people are to be told. You must tell my mother, Gadadhara, Chandrasekhara, Brahmananda and my dear Mukunda.'

That day the kirtans were blissful and more devotees came to gaze at Vishvambhar, drinking in his beauty. None except Nityananda and the five knew he was going to leave them that night. Each person present brought a flower garland to offer their Lord. One by one he called them forward so he could receive their garlands, and in return he lovingly placed a garland around each one's neck. Surrounded by a sea of bright faces he felt boundless love as they floated in an ocean of bliss. Looking at all these souls so dear to him, with tender love he spoke to them.

'Talk of Krishna, worship Krishna, sing Krishna's name. Think only of Krishna. If you love me, sing of Krishna and no one else. Whether asleep or awake, or while eating your meals, think only of Krishna day and night, and with your mouths speak only of Him.'

After speaking these final words, Vishvambhar told them all to go home. They were unaware of why he had spoken in the way he had, and full of joy they were about to leave for their beds. Just then, however, Sridhara appeared at the end of his long day carrying a large squash. Beaming with pleasure he offered it to his master.

'Sridhara, where did you find this?' laughed Vishvambhar, while inwardly he thought, 'Tomorrow I will not be here. I must accept this last offering and eat it tonight.' Someone else had brought some milk, so he asked his mother to prepare a meal.

'Cook the squash together with the milk, that will be good.'

It was late in the night by the time the kirtan drew to a close and they all sat down to eat. Once all was complete Vishvambhar sent them home. By the time all those in the household had gone to bed only two hours of darkness remained. Vishvambhar lay down and pretended to sleep. Soon all was quiet. In the darkness he opened his eyes, took a deep breath and sat up ready to depart. Beside him Gadadhara stirred. Aware that his master was leaving, he rose to accompany him.

'I go alone, Gadadhara. That is my wish,' whispered Vishvambhar.

Silently he moved to the door. On the threshold his mother sat on the ground waiting for him with aching heart. He sank down beside her, embraced her tightly, and spoke softly many things; how from birth she had taught him all he knew; how she had filled his life with joy; and how he could never repay her love.

'The Supreme Lord brings us together, and by his will we are separated. Who can understand his ways? I will return.'

Saci listened unable to speak as tears flowed silently down her cheeks. He placed his hand on her heart and gave her his final words of assurance.

'You are very dear to me. I am with you always.'

Taking the dust from her feet and placing it on his head, he walked around her with folded hands and disappeared into the night.

Dawn crept through the air. Saci sat motionless where her son had left her. Devotees began to stir, and some came to see Vishvambhar. They found Saci outside his door.

'Mother, why do you sit here?' spoke gentle Srivasa. At first she gave no answer, only tears. Then she found her voice.

'My fathers, the possessions of Vishnu belong to his devotees. Now you can all do with me as you like, for my Lord has left me.'

The devotees were stunned. Some whispered that Vishvambhar had left them to become a sannyasi. As word spread they gave themselves over to weeping, laying their heads on one another's shoulders, lying on the floor, sitting in corners with their heads in their hands. Hearing their sobbing, others came to find out what had happened. Soon all of Navadvipa heard the news and the whole town was in shock. Even those who had mocked him wept in remorse, falling to the ground.

'What a chance we have missed!' they cried out. 'We were sinners and did not understand his greatness.'

VISHVAMBHAR SPED TO THE GANGES and swam to the opposite shore, then hurried along the road to reach Katwa in time for late afternoon. There, as arranged, he was met by his five companions: Nityananda, Gadadhara, Mukunda, Chandrashekhara and Brahmananda. Together they went to Kesava Bharati and explained why they had come. When he learned he was being asked to offer sannyasa to the young Vishvambhar he was dismayed. He was reluctant to invest such a beautiful young man on the threshold of life with the ancient order of renunciation.

Crowds began to materialise as word spread of the famous Vishvambhar's presence and his intention to become a sannyasi. They looked on in awe as his companions chanted and danced with abandon. Seeing Vishvambhar's beauty people were sorry that he should be giving up the world at his tender age.

'How will his wife and mother continue without him?' said the women as they wept. 'How will they even stay alive?'

The kirtan came to an end. Vishvambhar sat before Kesava Bharati and humbly begged him to help him become a true servant of Krishna. The venerable sannyasi felt completely unqualified to initiate such an exalted person, but he was at last persuaded. So night fell and they rested.

In the morning a large crowd encircled their beloved Lord to watch the ceremony. A barber was brought forward and sat facing Vishvambhar, ready to shave his long curling hair. Tearfully the barber took his razor in his trembling hand and raised it to the tumbling locks. Hearing cries of dismay from the crowd and the wailing of women, he could go no further. Some even fainted. Vishvambhar was undeterred. He jumped to his feet, asked Mukunda to sing, and led everyone in chanting. Dancing with them, he swayed and trembled with ecstasy, weeping streams of tears and lifting the crowd into his mood of love for Krishna.

After some time they forgot their sadness and order was restored. While Mukunda continued singing, Vishvambhar again sat before the barber. He spoke some gentle words in his ear, giving him the strength to do his work. One by one the Lord's glistening locks fell to the ground, each treasured by some fortunate devotee. His head was anointed with sandalwood oil and all gasped to see him glow with a new beauty.

The initiation ceremony began. Kesava Bharati was unsure how to initiate the divine being whom he now believed to be before him, so Vishvambhar leaned forward and whispered into his ear the mantra for sannyasa initiation, prompting him to proceed. By doing this, in effect he made Kesava Bharati his disciple. All the elderly monk had to do was whisper the same mantra back to Vishvambhar and the formality was complete.

Vishvambhar donned new saffron cloth and was given a sannyasa staff and alms pot. Standing before the multitude, crying tears of ecstasy, his beauty shone for all to see.

Finally came the choice of name. The normal custom would be for an initiated sannyasi to adopt the name of his guru, in this case Bharati. But Kesava Bharati was reluctant to give this name to so unique and exalted a person as his disciple. So he searched his heart for a suitable name and was given divine guidance.

'You will inspire the whole world to chant Krishna's name and you will make all who hear you come alive, *chaitanya*, with the sound of chanting. Therefore I name you Sri Krishna Chaitanya.' These words were greeted with joyful cries of 'Hari!'

The new sannyasi liked his name and bowed before his initiator with gratitude. Everyone thought the name was perfect. The barber, still weeping, was congratulated. From that day he abandoned his profession and never shaved another head. The elderly monk put aside his staff and gave himself over to dancing. For the first time he experienced what it was to dance in ecstasy and cry for Krishna. After this day he became a changed man, always remembering Krishna. Many souls joined their kirtan and were blessed with the same good fortune.

So it was, amid joyous confusion, at the end of his twenty-fourth year, Vishvambhar became the glorious and dazzling sannyasi, Sri Krishna Chaitanya, and prepared to embark on his mission to preach the glories of the holy name of Krishna to people everywhere.

As the sun rose on a new day the young sannyasi said farewell to Keshava Bharati and thanked him for his momentous service. He walked westwards followed by a large crowd, many weeping at the prospect of losing him. Now that he had given up the world, his intention was to travel to Vrindavan.

He went along the path, dancing and ceaselessly singing Krishna's names. From time to time, overcome by ecstatic emotions, he sat by the path and wept. Wherever he stopped people crowded round, and hearing his sobs felt their hearts would break. Nityananda asked him to bless them, and sent them home. With only his four friends for company, Krishna Chaitanya entered Radhadesh, the region on the western bank of the Ganges.

For three days the saffron-robed Chaitanya wandered in Radhadesh. In his trance of divine love he believed he was on his way to Vrindavan. In reality, Nityananda succeeded in directing him in a half-circle, bringing him back toward Shantipur where he could meet his devotees one last time.

They came to the bank of the Ganges.

'Here is the Yamuna River that flows through Vrindavan,' Nityananda told him. 'You have only to follow the course of the river and you will soon reach Krishna's home.'

Chaitanya heard these words with joy, believing them to be true, and asked that a message be carried back to Navadvipa.

'Tell the Vaishnavas I am going to Vrindavan to find Krishna. Tell them not to be unhappy, for I love all of them birth after birth.' In his ecstasy he followed the river.

Nityananda gave Chandrasekhar a message in which he told Saci and the devotees to come to Advaita's house in Shantipur. There they would have a final meeting with her son. Chandrasekhar hurried to Navadvipa. When he arrived he found everyone had come together to comfort mother Saci, all weeping and chanting Krishna's names. He told them about Nityananda's plan, and encouraged them all to come with him to Shantipur. There for the last time they would be able to see their beloved Vishvambar before he left Navadvipa forever.

While Chaitanya continued on his way, Nityananda went ahead to Advaita's house. There he persuaded Advaita to bring a boat to meet his Lord who was approaching along the bank.

To his surprise Chaitanya saw Advaita approaching.

'Advaita! You too are here in Vrindavan?'

'Wherever you are, Lord, there is Vrindavan,' replied Advaita, relieved to find his beloved Vishvambhar. 'Even here on the bank of the Ganges. Now come with me to my home, where everyone is waiting for you.' Realising he had been tricked, Chaitanya agreed to board the boat.

At Advaita's house a wonderful meal had been prepared with many delicious foodstuffs. Since he was now a sannyasi Chaitanya wanted to renounce all comforts, eat only plain food and behave as a true mendicant. But Advaita had long wanted to receive Vishvambhar at his home and offer him a splendid feast befitting the Lord of the universe. So he sat Chaitanya down beside Nityananda and made him eat sumptuously, then led him to a comfortable bed and massaged his feet. Chaitanya accepted all this in good humour in the company of his two dear friends.

People in Navadvipa felt they had lost their glorious Vishvambhar, but now they received news of his initiation ceremony at Katwa, they were eager to meet him in his new dress as the renounced sannyasi Sri Krishna Chaitanya. Saci, who had fasted and wept for days, also wanted to meet her son in his new role. Even his former critics, the ones who had driven him to adopt sannyasa, experienced a change of heart and wanted to see him again. So a great tide of eager souls set out from Navadvipa in the direction of Shantipur. In their thousands they congregated around Advaita's house, hoping for a glimpse of Sri Chaitanya and loudly chanting Krishna's names.

When the meal was ended and Advaita's desires had been satifisfied, Chaitanya heard the great crowd chanting outside and went onto the veranda to show himself. He saw a vast gathering, numberless devotees stretching as far as the eye could see. He was astonished. The people beheld their beautiful young sannyasi and a great cry went up.

'Save us! Save us!' they cried, falling full length on their faces in the dust.

Among them were close friends who stepped forward to embrace him. Advaita began to sing with Nityananda and Haridas, and as darkness fell he joined them. A tumultuous kirtan enveloped them all in which his loving feelings for Krishna increased more and more until he fell helpless to the ground. Mukunda came and sat beside him singing sweet verses about Radharani's love for Krishna, so sending him still deeper into ecstasy. He lost all control of his body and mind and his devotees became anxious for his welfare. Advaita took him inside and made him lie down, while the chanting outside was suspended for the remainder of the night.

The following day Saci arrived from Navadvipa. When he saw his mother, Krishna Chaitanya fell to the floor before her and touched her feet. Seeing him for the first time without his beautiful curling hair, she looked in his face with tear-filled eyes.

'Do not be cruel to me, as your elder brother was,' she pleaded, kissing and caressing him. 'He left home and never returned or sent me news. If the same happens with you I will surely die.'

'Mother dear, this body belongs to you. Whatever you ask I will obey.'

Saci took charge of the cooking for her son and all his company. Thus Chaitanya stayed with Advaita for ten days, and during this time they discussed his future. It was decided, with the approval of Saci, that he should not go to Vrindavan, which was too far away. Instead he would stay in Jagannath Puri, the great holy city of Orissa. Puri stood on the shore of the Bay of Bengal three hundred miles south of Navadvipa and was home to the majestic Jagannath, Lord of the Universe, the form of Krishna revered throughout Orissa. News could travel between there and Navadvipa, devotees could visit him and from there he might also return to visit them in Navadvipa.

During those last few days in Bengal, their sharing of emotions reached new heights. Devotees got the chance to spend time with their Lord in the day, and at night to join him in ecstatic chanting and dancing. In those kirtans he manifested his loving ecstasies without restraint, leaping in the air, rolling on the ground, weeping and embracing his friends. On the final day he sat on Vishnu's altar in the midst of everyone and showed for the last time his glory as Lord of Lords.

'I am Krishna, I am Balarama and I am Rama,' he declared. 'I am Vishnu, Brahma and Shiva. Countless universes emanate from me. I kill the demons and protect my devotees. You, my dear devotees, are one with me. You are my father, mother, friend, son and brother. You are with me birth after birth and I am never separated from you, not even for a second.'

One last time they went to the Ganges to bathe, then sat together for a final meal. In the centre sat Chaitanya and Nityananda. Seing them together everyone was reminded of Krishna and Balarama eating lunch in the forest with their cowherd friends.

Early next morning, Chaitanya said farewell to his mother, bowing at her feet one last time. Then he set off for Jagannath Puri, taking with him Nityananda, Mukunda and two other companions. Many followed him, but after a short time he stopped and turned to them.

'I must go now, but in a while I will come back to visit you. Please do not be unhappy. Go to your homes and always chant Krishna's names. I will never leave you.' Then he spoke to Advaita. 'My dear Advaita, I depend upon you to guide the devotees. Please see that my mother is taken care of.'

With these words Sri Krishna Chaitanya embraced Advaita and quickly left, heading south with his four friends. His devotees, overwhelmed by grief, cried and fell to the ground. Then, comforting one another, they returned to their homes.

Book Two

WORLD

7

THE GOLDEN SANNYASI

K RISHNA CHAITANYA WAS AT LAST FREE to embark on
life as a sannyasi. His path lay south toward Jagannath
Puri. On the way he and his companions would pass
through difficult territory patrolled by Muslim forces. They
carried no money, so as not to attract thieves, and because
Chaitanya wanted them to depend entirely on Krishna for
food and shelter. Each night they stayed in someone's home.

As he travelled, he hardly knew if it was day or night or
where the path lay. He was absorbed in thoughts of Krishna,
and of how he would soon see his Lord in the form of the
deity Jagannath. They followed the Ganges and came to the
town of Chatrabhoga, where the river divided into many
streams called the Mouths of the Ganges, before spilling
into the Bay of Bengal. Here Chaitanya was greeted by the
governor Ramachandra Khan, who invited him and his
friends into his home and offered to guide them safely
through the dangerous territory ahead.

In the depth of night they were led down to the Ganges where a boat had been made ready. Climbing aboard they slid into the smooth-flowing waters of Mother Ganges. In the darkness Mukunda began to sing Krishna's names as shadows drifted by along the banks. The boatman, fearing crocodiles and pirates, begged Mukunda to sing quietly lest he attract attention.

'Have no fear!' said Chaitanya. 'We are protected by the sound of Krishna's names.'

As dawn broke they reached the borders of Orissa. The boatman steered them ashore at Sri Prayag Ghat, where Sri Krishna Chaitanya first set foot on the soil of Orissa. They bathed in the Ganges, then entered the temple of Shiva to pay their respects. The custom was for a sannyasi to gather alms, so Chaitanya told the others to stay at the temple while he went from house to house begging for rice and vegetables. All who saw him were captivated by his effulgent beauty, and fell under his spell, so that very soon he returned with his cloth overflowing. When they saw how much he had collected his friends broke into broad smiles—evidently they would not starve on this journey. After cooking and eating, as darkness fell they listened while Mukunda sang them into the night.

On the road next morning they came to a tollgate where the collector demanded money to let them pass. Thinking he would be prevented from reaching Jagannath's temple, Chaitanya began to cry. The collector was moved by his tears and let him pass, but insisted the others must pay. When

Chaitanya saw his companions barred, he sat alone by the road and wept even more. His cries were enough to melt anyone's heart. Bowing before this beautiful young monk and himself crying, the collector let them all through.

Moving onward through Orissa for several days, they reached the bank of the River Bharginadi, close to Jagannath Puri. Chaitanya had with him his danda, the bamboo staff that was the symbol of his sannyasa order. This staff had been entrusted to Nityananda, who did not appreciate it because he had never wanted Chaitanya to become a sannyasi, and to his mind the burden of such an outward symbol was entirely unnecessary for his exalted friend. In a mood of disgust, he broke the staff into three pieces and cast it into the river. Wanting his danda, Chaitanya asked Nityananda where it was. When he heard it had been broken and thrown away he was angry.

'This danda was my only companion, and now you have destroyed it. I will go on without you.'

He strode ahead on his own, walking quickly and purposefully. In the distance he soon saw the red flag of Jagannath flying in the sea breeze, fixed to the pinnacle of the great temple whose monumental stonework towered above the waving palms. With mounting excitement he hurried on, anticipating the sight of the wonderful Lord Jagannath, Krishna himself, served in his gigantic form by hundreds of priests and worshipped by countless pilgrims. Behind him trailed his companions, anxious not to lose sight of their master.

AN EFFULGENT YOUNG SANNYASI arrived alone at the Lion Gate of the great temple of Puri. The guards had never seen a monk with such personal beauty and godlike appearance. They watched him pass through the gateway and across the outer courtyard, seeming to float rather than walk, oblivious of his surroundings as if in a dream.

The golden figure disappeared into the engulfing shadows of the inner temple. Beyond the reach of daylight in the innermost chamber he saw before him, illuminated by the flickering glow of oil lamps, attended by priests moving silently in the darkness, the immense form of Jagannath. He stopped motionless, his gaze mesmerised by Jagannath's huge face, his great circular eyes and his broad red smile. The deity's two extended arms were marked with the signs of conch and disc, symbols of Vishnu's power and mercy. Jagannath was Krishna, Lord of the Universe, and beside him equally immense stood the forms of his sister Subhadra and his mighty brother Balarama.

For a moment the golden sannyasi stood mesmerised, his body trembling as tears flooded his cheeks. His breath came in gasps as he tried to call the name of Jagannath, then with a cry he fell to the floor. Guards rushed forward and would have handled him roughly, but were stopped by a diminutive and dignified man who stepped from the shadows. Stooping, he studied the golden figure sprawled at his feet. He saw at once by his noble features and luminous aura that this was no ordinary man. He sat down on the stone floor beside him, shielding him from the guards, and waiting for him to regain consciousness. As he waited he noticed with alarm that the sannyasi did not appear to be breathing. He called for help and had him carried to a side room, where he held a piece of cotton to the young man's nostrils and saw it move slightly. Relieved, he concluded that this person was in a deep trance, in which he saw all the symptoms of the most profound spiritual rapture. With great care, helped by temple attendants, he brought this unknown monk to the safety of his house.

This man so conscientiously reaching out to help was Sarvabhauma Bhattacarya, the most respected elder of Puri. He was celebrated in his day as the greatest authority and teacher of the philosophy of Advaita Vedanta. People came from all over India to learn from him the sublime teaching of the unity of all life in Brahman, pure spirit.

NITYANANDA REACHED THE MAIN GATE of the temple with the other devotees and began enquiring—had anyone seen a tall young sannyasi who shone with inner light? Temple attendants told them excitedly of the appearance of a strange sannyasi who had fainted before Jagannath. Just then Mukunda recognised among the attendants his old friend Gopinath, who had visited Navadvipa and himself become a devotee of Sri Krishna Chaitanya. Gopinath was now a resident of Puri. They exchanged embraces and Gopinath led the group to Sarvabhauma's house. As they walked he explained all that had happened. Soon they were shown inside and breathed sighs of relief to see their master lying unconscious but cared for in a secluded place.

Sarvabhauma welcomed the devotees and assured them their beloved lord was in safe hands. Then they allowed him to guide them to the great temple. Since the mighty Jagannath was proprietor of the town of Jagannath Puri, they needed to go before him to offer their prayers before doing anything else. So they stood blissfully before Lord Jagannath and received flower garlands from the priests.

When they returned they found Chaitanya lying peacefully where they had left him, still breathing only slightly. They gathered round him to sing Krishna's names, as they had done many times before. Soon his eyes opened and he looked around him.

'Welcome to my home, master,' said Sarvabhauma respectfully. 'You are my guest and I count myself fortunate. Now if you are feeling recovered please take your bath, then I will feed you and your friends the food offered to Lord Jagannath.'

Gopinath led Chaitanya and his devotees on a short walk to the long sandy beach, customary bathing place for the people of Puri. Palms and sand dunes stretched in both directions and gentle waves lapped the shore. After swimming in the healing waters they returned refreshed to Sarvabhauma's house, where their host served them a magnificent lunch. He then came forward to introduce himself properly and find out who his special guest was.

'*Namo Narayanaya*,' intoned the elder, using the traditional words to greet a sannyasi. These words addressed a person as the Supreme Narayana, as one who had realised his unity with God and all beings.

'*Krishna matir astu*,' Chaitanya responded, meaning, 'Place your mind upon Krishna.' By this exchange they each identified themselves, Sarvabhauma as a philosopher of Advaita who taught that all beings are one with God, and Chaitanya as a devotee of Krishna, who taught that the perfection of life was to be the loving servant of God.

Sarvabhauma was himself originally from Navadvipa, and as they talked he discovered that Chaitanya's grandfather had been a close friend of his own father. Learning this inspired in him a fatherly affection toward this dazzling young monk. He made arrangements for him to stay in his house as long as he liked, and delegated his brother-in-law Gopinath to look after all his needs. Further, he decided it was his duty to teach his adopted nephew and give him the benefit of his personal instruction in Vedanta philosophy so he could be well grounded in his renunciation of the world, and safe from the temptations that might assail a handsome and charismatic young monk. When Gopinath heard of Sarvabhauma's offer to teach his worshipable master, he was indignant.

'Sri Krishna Chaitanya is no ordinary human being: he is the Supreme Lord himself. Why should he need instruction from you?'

'My dear Gopinath, I readily accept Sri Krishna Chaitanya as a wonderful devotee of Krishna, but where is the evidence that he is a divine avatar?' responded Sarvabhauma. Whereupon Gopinath hotly debated whether or not Chaitanya was in fact an incarnation of God. His arguments did not convince the teacher, who insisted on inviting Chaitanya to receive instruction from him, suggesting that they meet soon at the great Jagannath temple. Chaitanya did not resist.

'Sarvabhauma Bhattacarya is kind to me,' he said, waving aside Gopinath's objections. 'He just wants to help me be a good sannyasi. Where is the harm?' So he accepted Sarvabhauma's offer to teach him the Vedanta Sutras. One day not long afterwards they sat together in a quiet corner of the precincts of the temple and instructions began.

SARVABHAUMA, IN RESPECT FOR his distinguished student's status as a sannyasi, arranged a raised seat for him, and sat himself on the floor at Chaitanya's feet.

'Now we will begin our lessons. For your own good, listen to me recite the Vedanta with the commentaries of the great Shankara, and learn from what I say.' With this he began lecturing. His lectures spread over seven days, while

Chaitanya listened obediently. When the teacher got to the end of his teaching he was perplexed.

'For seven days you have listened in silence. Why have you not spoken? Have you understood anything I've said?'

'I am a fool,' replied Chaitanya. 'I am not attracted to the intricacies of Vedanta philosophy. But because you tell me it is my duty as a sannyasi, I am trying my best to follow what you say.'

'If you don't understand what I'm saying, then why not ask me to explain?'

'I understand the sutras themselves—their meaning is self-luminous—but Shankara's commentary obscures them like a cloud. It seems to me that his commentary avoids the direct meaning of the sutras and instead interprets them indirectly.'

He went on to explain the sutras in a simple and direct way that didn't touch upon Sarvabhauma's elaborate interpretations. He concluded by saying that the great Shankara's commentary, far from clarifying the truth, misled followers of the Vedas into thinking that God is impersonal, and in so doing obstructed their natural faith in a personal God. Sarvabhauma resisted Chaitanya's words with more arguments of his own, but he was soon overcome by the truth, beauty and harmony of what he heard.

Sri Chaitanya recited a verse from the *Srimad Bhagavatam* describing one who has become fully self-satisfied. Such a perfect soul is called 'atmarama', one whose innermost self is saturated with deep joy. The *Bhagavatam* says this person has lost all attraction to this illusory world of *maya*, yet still desires to serve the beautiful personality of Godhead. This is because Krishna is beyond the illusion. All else may be illusion, but Krishna is real and love for Krishna is everlasting love, not part of the illusion. Such love belongs to the eternal spirit.

Sarvabhauma asked Chaitanya to explain the verse in detail. He agreed, but first invited the learned teacher to give his own explanations. Sarvabhauma explained the Sanskrit verse in nine different ways, then listened dumbfounded as his supposed student gave sixty-four further explanations of the verse, without touching on his teacher's interpretations. Hearing these, the teacher realised he was in the presence of an extraordinary being. His heart went through a profound change. Denouncing his pride he implored for mercy.

Sri Chaitanya showed Sarvabhauma a vision of himself as Vishnu, then as Krishna playing a flute. When Sarvabhauma saw these wonderful visions he stretched full length on the floor in love and adoration, holding Chaitanya's feet and weeping.

At last he spoke.

'Today I have found the thief who stole my heart.'

'Rise, Sarvabhauma,' said his new divine master, placing his hand on Sarvabhauma's head. 'I have shown you this vision because you are very dear to me. For many lifetimes you have been my devoted servant, and I came to Puri just to deliver you.'

With folded hands, weeping and trembling, Sarvabhauma sang beautiful Sanskrit prayers in praise of Sri Krishna Chaitanya. Before they parted, his Lord asked that as long as he remained on Earth, Sarvabhauma told no one of his vision.

Next day Sarvabhauma's pride had evaporated. He came to Chaitanya with a question. He fell at his master's feet.

'In offering devotional service to the Lord, what is the most important practice?'

Chaitanya gave him the same instruction he had first given to Suklambara in Navadvipa:

> *'The holy name, the holy name, the holy name of Krishna is all you need. In this age of Kali nothing else, nothing else, nothing else will bring spiritual success.'*

As master of the reputed Sarvabhauma, Chaitanya came to be known as Mahaprabhu, the Great Master. His devotees were overjoyed at Sarvabhauma's transformation. Mukunda heard the Sanskrit verses he had composed and inscribed two of them on the outer wall of his house for all to see. These two verses were learned by Chaitanya's followers:

> *I surrender to the Supreme Lord, who has appeared in this world as the ocean of mercy, Sri Krishna Chaitanya, to teach knowledge, detachment and devotional service to himself.*
>
> *The ancient science of devotional service was lost over the course of time, and Sri Krishna Chaitanya has come to revive it. May my consciousness, like a honeybee, find shelter at his lotus feet.*

The people of Jagannath Puri heard how deeply the young sannyasi from Bengal had influenced their most respected citizen, and watched him as he walked about their town blissfully chanting Krishna's name, radiating love to all who saw him. They already had their sacred Jagannath, Lord of the Universe, whom they worshipped in the great temple—now they saw a second Jagannath among them. They called Chaitanya the moving Jagannath. One Jagannath stood in the temple to receive their worship; the other moved among them. Seeing Sri Chaitanya's personal beauty, their hearts were captivated and they thought of him constantly.

ONE EVENING BY THE LIGHT of the full moon, in the company of his friends Mahaprabhu went to the palm-fringed seashore. An expanding group of companions had been gathering around him since he arrived in Puri. Cooled by the sea breeze, they sat together on the beach to sing and talk of Krishna. The moon's rays sparkled on the ocean waves, and this beautiful sight reminded Mahaprabhu of the Yamuna River as she flowed past the forest of Vrindavan. In ecstasy he stayed on the beach all night long, singing to Krishna and dancing. When he danced, tumultuous emotions swept through his body. He shed tears or laughed, embraced his friends and rolled in the sand. They cherished the memories of these occasions, when their beloved Lord made the ocean glorious.

After being in Puri for little more than a month, Mahaprabhu called together his close companions. Taking their hands he spoke in deep humility.

'You are all dear to me. You brought me here to the temple of Jagannath, and I never want to lose your company. But now I ask you one special favour. Let me go on pilgrimage to South India. There I will look for my older brother Vishvarup. I wish to travel alone as a sannyasi, but I will soon return.'

Speaking for them all, Nityananda protested.

'Dear Lord, if you must go then at least take a few of us with you.'

But Mahaprabhu was firm. He could only be persuaded to take with him a single companion, a simple man named Krishnadas who would look after his personal needs. So it was agreed, and next day he took leave of Sarvabhauma.

'After many lifetimes I have found you,' cried the elderly teacher, 'Yet now you are leaving me.' To please Sarvabhauma, Mahaprabhu agreed to stay at his house a few days longer. When it was at last time for him to leave, Sarvabhauma made a special request.

'In the town of Vidyanagara by the River Godavari you will find Ramananda Raya. He is the governor of Madras. Although he may appear preoccupied with material affairs, he is a loving devotee of Krishna with deep understanding of devotional service. Please meet him—I am sure you will appreciate his company.' Mahaprabhu promised he would find him.

When he saw his master leave, Sarvabhauma was so overcome with emotion that he fainted and had to be helped back to his house. Others followed their newfound teacher as far as he would allow them, then they too were left behind, weeping as they watched him go. Although he greatly missed his friends, Mahaprabhu was determined. With joy in his heart he walked purposefully toward the South. Only Krishnadas walked with him.

8

MEETING BY THE RIVER

SINGING JOYFULLY, MAHAPRABHU followed the path. A favourite chant was always on his lips:

Krishna Krishna Krishna Krishna Krishna Krishna Krishna he
Krishna Krishna Krishna Krishna Krishna Krishna Krishna he
Krishna Krishna Krishna Krishna Krishna Krishna raksa mam
Krishna Krishna Krishna Krishna Krishna Krishna pahi mam
Rama Raghava Rama Raghava Rama Raghava raksa mam
Krishna Kesava Krishna Kesava Krishna Kesava pahi mam

'O Krishna, protect me and maintain me.
O Rama, descendant of Raghu, protect me.
Krishna, killer of the Kesi demon, maintain me.'

While he travelled in the South, Sri Chaitanya manifested powers he had hitherto kept hidden. As he passed through each village, people followed him and joined him in chanting Krishna's names. He would embrace them, transforming their hearts and overwhelming them with love for God.

These people returned to their villages where they continued chanting, and whoever heard their chanting sang with them and also became devotees of Krishna. Through his blessings, Krishna consciousness spread wherever he went.

One such village was Kurmakshetra, where stood an ancient temple dedicated to the avatar of Vishnu named Kurma, who in the form of a cosmic turtle supported the entire universe when the gods and demons churned the Milk Ocean. Here lived a humble brahmin who invited Mahaprabhu into his home and washed his feet, then cooked for him and shared the sanctified remnants of the meal among his family.

'Lord, you have blessed me and my family today,' said the brahmin. 'Please let me leave my home and family and come with you. I can no longer tolerate the waves of misery caused by material life.' When he heard these words, Mahaprabhu was firm. He told the brahmin never to speak like that and taught him an important lesson.

His order to all *'Stay at home and always chant the name of Krishna. Tell whomever you meet the teachings of Krishna. By my order become guru and free your people.'*

Wherever he received hospitality during his travels, Mahaprabhu stayed long enough to give the householders the same essential teaching.

HE REACHED THE BANK of the River Godavari, near
Vidyanagara. There he bathed in her sacred waters and rested
beneath a tree. As he sat beside the river, remembering the
Yamuna in Vrindavan and quietly chanting Krishna's names,
he saw a large group approaching. A man of importance,
carried in a palanquin and attended by musicians, priests and
servants, came to the river to bathe and perform a Vedic rite.

Mahaprabhu understood this was Ramananda Raya,
governor of Madras, the very man Sarvabhauma had wanted
him to meet. From a distance the governor saw the saffron-
robed sannyasi with golden skin and eyes like lotus petals.
He came over to pay his respects, and as he approached he
found himself dazzled as if by the light of many suns. He
dropped to the ground before this effulgent figure, stretching
himself full length in the sand.

Mahaprabhu raised him to his feet and asked if he was
Ramananda Raya, whereupon the governor introduced
himself as Chaitanya's unworthy servant. He was given a
warm embrace. For a long time they held each other tight.
Although in this lifetime they had not met, they recognised
one another and deep feelings of love awoke in their hearts
as both of them wept.

Many of Ramananda's company were touched by the sight
of their master embracing this young sannyasi, and they
began to chant Krishna's names. The brahmins attending

Ramananda, however, although well educated in spiritual matters, did not appreciate what they saw. They disapproved of a sannyasi embracing a governor, and were unhappy to see Ramananda, who they knew to be a highly educated and intelligent man, apparently losing all composure and weeping like a child. Seeing their critical gaze, Mahaprabhu and Ramananda restrained their feelings and moved some distance away to sit and talk. They spoke first of Sarvabhauma, whose kindness Ramananda praised for sending Chaitanya to see a worldly man like him. Then they agreed they must meet alone as soon as possible. Fortunately a humble brahmin who lived nearby invited Mahaprabhu to stay in his home, and they decided to meet there.

That evening Ramananda, with just one attendant, came to the brahmin's house. There he and Mahaprabhu withdrew to a private room and entered deep conversation.

REVELATION OF HIGHEST LOVE

IN THE COMPANY OF RAMANANDA, Mahaprabhu took the role of student and placed a series of questions. He began by asking him to recite a verse from scripture about the ultimate goal of life.

Ramananda was a governor committed to the people's welfare, so he replied with a Sanskrit verse from the *Vishnu Purana* that prescribed the general good of human society. The verse spoke of *vishnu aradhyate*, the worship of Vishnu.

'One should do one's moral duty with the intention to worship Vishnu, and so awaken one's God consciousness.'

He meant that if people carry out their social duties with God in mind, in time they will be rewarded with increased understanding of God.

'Go deeper,' urged Mahaprabhu.

Ramananda recited a verse from the *Bhagavad Gita*.

'Whatever you do, whatever you eat, whatever you offer or give away, and whatever hardship you undergo, do it all for Me.'

By this he suggested not only that people should do their religious duty—but they should do it for the sake of Krishna.

Again Mahaprabhu asked him to go further. Ramananda recited another verse from the *Gita*, in which Krishna recommends giving up duties altogether and simply surrendering to him.

'Abandon all kinds of religion and surrender to Me alone. I will free you from all sinful reactions. Do not fear.'

Still Mahaprabhu demanded more. He wanted to hear of positive spiritual engagement rather than renunciation. Ramananda went on to speak a verse from the *Srimad Bhagavatam*.

'The Lord is conquered by those who, regardless of their position in life, simply hear about him from his devotees.'

'Yes,' said Mahaprabhu, 'this is right.'

All his life he had taught that in this age people should try to reach God simply by devotion. They did not need to perform pious work, pursue knowledge or renounce this world. They could stay in whatever condition they may be and just hear about Krishna from his devotees. So they would learn to love him.

Once Mahaprabhu accepted this sublime principle he urged Ramananda to keep going deeper in exploring devotion to Krishna. Being so inspired, Ramananda went on to describe how love for God is the highest goal of life, and how a soul's loving relationship with Krishna can grow through successive stages of intimacy, starting with humble adoration, moving to joyful friendship, then to the love of a mother for her child, and ultimately manifesting in conjugal love, the sweet union between two lovers.

Ramananda Raya had deep knowledge of the inner world of pure love for Krishna, but no one had ever asked such penetrating questions as Mahaprabhu now put to him. He felt his tongue loosened and made to vibrate like a stringed instrument. For successive nights they met and talked of the love between Krishna and his devotees. They were like explorers gathering rare minerals and gems from hidden depths.

They talked of how Krishna responds to his devotee's wishes: for the one who wants to love him as a mother loves her child, he will transform into a baby as he did for his mother Yasoda when he lived in Vrindavan. For another he might be a childhood friend and spend all day playing games together or herding cows. And those who want to be with him as lover can share in his everlasting loving pastimes with Radha and her forest girlfriends. Ramananda described the path leading to this highest perfection as following in the footsteps of the cowherd girls, drawn by the sound of Krishna's flute to dance with him in the moonlit night in his enchanted forest home.

Their talks reached the supreme expression of Krishna's love: his union with the Goddess Radha. She is the ultimate embodiment of Krishna's purest compassion and ecstasy. When Ramananda began to describe her he entered the realms of spiritual rapture. In the darkness of the night, while all around them slept, he and Mahaprabhu tasted mysteries unknown to this world as they invoked her presence.

As Ramananda spoke, inspired to go ever deeper, he reached places not accessible to any but the most blessed souls. At last they could go no further, and the door opened to Mahaprabhu's greatest secret.

Before Ramananda's eyes, Sri Chaitanya transformed into Krishna playing his flute. Ramananda saw Krishna's bluish hue was suffused with the golden lustre of Radha, and so at last was revealed to him the innermost truth: that Chaitanya was both Radha and Krishna combined in one person. When Ramananda saw this he fell into a trance.

His Lord gently brought him round and told him no one had ever seen this form, and it should remain a secret between them.

Then the Golden One embraced him.

FOR TEN DAYS they stayed by the River Godavari and each night they talked—but still they felt they had hardly begun. When the time came for Ramananda to leave, Sri Chaitanya invited him to move permanently to Jagannath Puri where they would be able to meet every day and spend their time speaking of Krishna. From that time Ramananda began to plan his withdrawal from government service so that he could devote the remainder of his days to being with Mahaprabhu in Puri.

ON HIS CONTINUING TRAVELS Mahaprabhu visited holy sites across South India. Wherever he went he taught them about Krishna and changed the course of their lives.

During the four months of the rainy season Mahaprabhu stayed in the temple city of Rangakshetra. There he was a guest in the house of Venkata Bhatta, one of the chief priests of the great temple of Sri Rangam, largest Vishnu temple in India. Influenced by his presence, Venkata and his family developed lasting personal devotion for Krishna. Among them his son Gopal Bhatta, who at the time was a young boy, became a devout follower of Sri Chaitanya and later moved to Vrindavan. Many were blessed to hear from Mahaprabhu during his stay and to receive from him the benediction of Krishna's names.

In the city lived a faithful brahmin who visited the temple every day. Each morning he did his best to chant the verses of love and wisdom spoken by Krishna to his friend Arjuna in the *Bhagavad Gita*. The brahmin was a simple man who could neither understand nor properly pronounce the Sanskrit verses. Some of the educated brahmins made fun of his efforts, but he was not deterred. One day Mahaprabhu came upon him chanting the verses of the Gita, and saw that he was trembling, his eyes filled with tears.

'What part of the *Gita* moves you so deeply?'

'Master, I do not understand Lord Krishna's words nor can I pronounce them properly, but I chant them because my guru instructed me to, and as I chant I see before me the image of beautiful Krishna, so kind to his friend Arjuna that he has taken the reins of his chariot and is teaching him. This image fills my heart with happiness and I can think of nothing else.'

'You are the one who truly knows the *Bhagavad Gita*,' said Mahaprabhu, embracing him. Upon receiving this embrace, the brahmin cried in astonishment, for before him he saw the very same Krishna whom he daily worshipped. After this he wanted to be with Mahaprabhu all the time. He visited him daily at Venkata's house, where he was personally taught many things. When the time came for Mahaprabhu to leave Rangakshetra he asked the brahmin to promise not to tell anyone the secret of his divine identity.

For two years Mahaprabhu continued his travels across South India. Moving from village to village he touched the hearts of fortunate souls everywhere, visited holy sites and taught about Krishna. He asked all those he taught to pass on to others what they had heard from him.

<blockquote>
His wish for all

'Whether you are a brahmin, a sannyasi or a householder, if you understand the truth about Krishna you can be a guru and teach others.'
</blockquote>

Wherever he went he inspired those who heard him to become devotees of Krishna, and he established the chanting of Krishna's holy names.

On his way back to Jagannath Puri he again spent several days with Ramananda in Vidyanagara and continued their mystical discussions. From there he returned by the same road on which he had left two years before.

He reached the edge of Puri, and sent Krishnadas ahead to tell Nityananda of his arrival. His friends hurried out to meet him, crying tears of joy. Together they took him to the temple of Jagannath, where Sarvabhauma fell at his feet. Mahaprabhu told Sarvabhauma that although he had travelled all over South India he had not found such a wonderful Vaishnava as Sarvabhauma. Mahaprabhu then went before Jagannath and danced in ecstasy surrounded by his friends, while the priests came out to give him garlands and sanctified food.

He was brought to Sarvabhauma's house where he bathed and ate. There he heard how, while he had been away, the King of Orissa had arranged a set of rooms for him in Kasi Misra's house. His friends took him to his new home where

Kasi Misra received him with reverence. In great affection they sat up with him all through the night, hearing the stories of his wonderful experiences in South India.

9

FESTIVALS OF LOVE

FOR TWO LONG YEARS the devotees in Bengal had been without their beloved Vishvambhar. In his absence, as he asked them, they continued with their kirtans, gathering in their homes or meeting at the houses of Srivasa and Advaita, and regularly meeting in public to perform street sankirtan. Hearing he had returned to Puri, in great eagerness they made preparations to come and see him.

Around this time Mahaprabhu was joined in Puri by three devoted souls who were to become his close personal companions. One was Svarupa Damodara, who became his personal assistant. They had been friends in Navadvipa, and after Chaitanya renounced the world Svarupa had gone to Varanasi where he himself took the order of sannyasa. Now they were re-united with great affection. Svarupa had profound knowledge of Vaishnava literature and special sensitivity to the transcendental emotions tasted by Mahaprabhu. He was able to respond to his moods in ways nobody else could, by singing from the devotional poems of Vidyapati, Chandidas and Jayadev.

A second companion was Govinda, who had been personal servant to their guru Isvara Puri. Before Isvara Puri left this world he had ordered Govinda to go to Puri and devote himself to Mahaprabhu's personal service.

The third was his special friend Gadadhara. The two of them had been friends since childhood and now they became inseparable, Gadadhara reading to Mahaprabhu daily from the *Srimad Bhagavatam*, bringing to life the stories of Krishna's loving exchanges with his devotees.

Many others were now joining their master in Puri, each possessing unique qualities and serving him in their own way. From all over the country they came to seek his shelter, as rivers flowing to the sea, and he gave them his lasting friendship, love and spiritual shelter.

The King of Orissa, Maharaja Prataparudra, was a powerful ruler hard pressed to defend Orissa from the Muslim ruler Husain Shah to the north in Bengal, and from the inroads of Krishnadev Raya to the south, whose armies presented a constant threat. Prataparudra was a military genius, as well as being a deeply religious man dedicated to the service of Jagannath. When he heard of Sri Chaitanya's presence in Puri, the king had been preoccupied with war. Now, having reached a halt in the fighting, he returned to his capital and immediately wanted to meet the great spiritual personality in their midst.

A king was expected to show honour to a sannyasi, and tradition required King Prataparudra to seek permission for an audience. He asked Sarvabhauma to arrange it, but was dismayed to learn that Mahaprabhu's strict vows of renunciation prevented him from keeping company with a king so caught up in affairs of the world. Sarvabhauma repeatedly implored Mahaprabhu to receive the king, but without success.

'The king may be a great devotee of Jagannath,' said Sri Chaitanya, 'but it would be dangerous for me to associate with him. If you persist with this suggestion I will leave this place.' Hearing these words, Sarvabhauma was afraid to say anything more. He pondered what to do.

Prataparudra had by now heard all about the glories of Mahaprabhu, and was more anxious than ever to meet him. When his request was again refused he became confused and despondent.

'If Mahaprabhu has appeared in this world to free even the most fallen souls like Jagai and Madhai, why will he not see me? Am I the only one not to receive his mercy? Without him my kingdom seems empty and useless.'

Sarvabhauma promised the king that since his devotion for Chaitanya was deep, he would surely soon be rewarded. He must be patient whilst a way was found to arrange a meeting. Hopes were raised when Ramananda Raya arrived in Puri with a great retinue of horses, elephants and soldiers. He was a worldly man, or at least he had been, yet he went straight to see Sri Chaitanya, and to everyone's surprise they embraced, shedding tears of love. Ramananda told Mahaprabhu that the king, wanting to please Sri Chaitanya, had allowed him to retire from government service and move to Puri.

'By this generous act he has served a devotee, and therefore Krishna is pleased,' assured Mahaprabhu. 'Krishna has said that a person devoted to him directly is not his devotee, but one who serves his devotee is best of all.'

Yet still Mahaprabhu did not agree to meet the king.

A large party of followers from Bengal arrived to see Chaitanya. He sent Svarupa Damodara and Govinda with garlands to greet them. The king watched their arrival with Sarvabhauma from the roof of his palace. He saw Govinda garland a venerable elder among the visitors and learned this was Advaita Acarya, respected leader of the devotee community in Bengal, a man revered by Chaitanya. He was struck by the appearance of all the visitors, and for the first time time heard their heartfelt singing.

'Never before have I heard the names of God sung with such single-minded absorption,' he marvelled. 'Nor have I witnessed such ecstatic love.'

The devotees streamed into Mahaprabhu's residence to see the one who had filled their thoughts all the time they had been apart. He was overjoyed to see his beloved friends. First he embraced Advaita with deep feeling, then Srivasa, then each one of them as he welcomed them to Kasi Misra's house. They all squeezed in, as he gave each one a garland, a place to sit and sandalwood paste to cool their foreheads.

Among them one remained outside, staying at a distance and lying prostrate in the road. This was Haridas, revered by all. Devotees begged him to come inside and join them, but he said he was not worthy to be so near the great temple of Jagannath.

'Let me have a solitary place nearby where I can stay and chant. That is all I wish for.'

Sri Chaitanya heard of Haridas's desire and was moved with love for him. He spoke to Kasi Misra.

'Here in your garden is a small cottage, secluded and quiet. Please give it to me.'

Having acquired this boon he sent everyone to bathe in the sea, while he went alone to meet Haridasa. He found him sitting by the road peacefully chanting the holy name. Seeing his lord approach, he fell before him full length in the dust. Mahaprabhu raised him gently in his arms, and they embraced with tears of love. He then led Haridas to the garden and showed him the simple cottage surrounded by flowers and blossoming trees.

'This room is for you. You have undergone many trials on Krishna's behalf in your life. Now you can stay close by me and chant all day. From here you can see the pinnacle of Jagannath's temple, and I will send you daily prasadam.'

Having accomplished this Mahaprabhu went to the beach where he sported with his friends amid the waves. Once they had bathed and eaten lunch, they visited the temple of Lord Jagannath. A great joyful kirtan took place, in which they danced and sang in four groups circling the outside of the temple. Sri Krishna Chaitanya danced in their midst, leaping high into the air, crying profuse tears and shivering in ecstasy. Sometimes he fell to the ground and Nityananda picked him up. The devotees were inspired to dance in unrestrained ecstasy, each one seeing Mahaprabhu looking only at them. None understood how this could be, yet all felt certain it was so. As each one came near he embraced them tightly while tears of love flowed from his eyes. The King and all who saw this extraordinary sankirtan were amazed.

THE TIME OF RATHAYATRA approached, bringing great excitement. The chariot festival of Jagannath was the high point of the year in Jagannath Puri. It had been held each year since ancient times, and attracted vast numbers of pilgrims. The name Jagannath, meaning Lord of the Universe, referred to Krishna, who was worshipped together with his sister Subhadra and his brother Balarama. Their three forms carved from wood were very large, requiring many servants to carry them. Although they were wooden they were considered pure spirit and were called *daru brahman*—spirit made of wood. Each summer the three huge forms were brought out of the temple and raised onto three enormous chariots to be pulled in procession down the main street of Puri to the Gundica temple a mile away. There they stayed for a week before returning in procession to the great temple of Jagannath. This was the Rathayatra Festival, an opportunity for all the people, who during the year may not be able to see Jagannath, to see him and receive his merciful gaze. It was said that anyone who saw the form of Jagannath during Rathayatra would be liberated from the cycle of birth and death.

In preparation for Rathayatra, as a special service to Jagannath, Mahaprabhu asked permission for himself and his followers to thoroughly clean the Gundica temple and make it ready for the arrival of Jagannath, Subhadra and Balarama. The King personally granted his wish, and on the chosen day Mahaprabhu gathered hundreds of followers, each with a water pot and broom, and together they made their way to the Gundica temple.

Once there he took personal charge. First he led everyone in sweeping, beginning with the main altar and fanning out through the temple and kitchens, into the courtyard and all the way to the edges of the compound. Each one tried to outdo the other in gathering as much dirt, leaves and twigs as they could. Once the whole temple had been thoroughly swept, Mahaprabhu led the way in sweeping a second time to make sure even the tiniest particles were collected. Only then did they begin to wash the temple. Hundreds of pots of water were brought from the nearby lake and thrown over the ceilings, walls and floors, beginning from the altar and working outward. Using his own outer garment as a cleaning cloth, Mahaprabhu polished the altar and wiped the floors.

While working, the devotees sang 'Hari!' and 'Krishna Krishna!' When the whole temple was thoroughly cleansed inside and out it was sparkling, cool and fresh, and the minds of the devotees felt as peaceful and purified as the temple. While Svarupa Damodara sang Mahaprabhu danced, his tears falling like raindrops. They joined him, dancing and singing with abandon.

Afterwards they bathed in the lake, then sat in a nearby garden to feast. From the great Jagannath temple enough food was brought to feed hundreds. Mahaprabhu sat beside Sarvabhauma, amid the laughter of all his friends.

'I used to spend my time debating with dry logicians,' said Sarvabhauma. 'Now I float in an ocean of friendship, surrounded by caring devotees.'

'And in your company, Sarvabhauma, we are all learning to love Krishna,' smiled Mahaprabhu.

Every year during the two weeks prior to Rathayatra, Jagannath remained hidden from view. Now on the eve of the festival he could again be seen. Sri Chaitanya had much missed seeing his Lord, so taking with him a group of devotees he went to the great temple. Entering the side room where Jagannath's food was offered, they caught a private glimpse of his beautiful form. Jagannath's enormous red-rimmed eyes blossomed like lotuses, his neck shone as a row of sapphires, and his broad smile spread sweet as nectar. Their eyes drank his beauty like bumblebees—they could not remove their gaze from his shining face. Mahaprabhu's eyes so filled with tears that when he looked at the Lord's face he saw only a blur.

Next morning the three colossal chariots waited in the road outside the main temple gate. Each had sixteen enormous wheels, supporting a high platform with hundreds of attendants, roofed by a brightly coloured silken canopy reaching to the sky. The sides of the wooden chariots were painted in vivid colours and festooned with banners, bells, gongs and mirrors. Their lofty canopies soared to golden pinnacles glittering in the morning sun, topped with multi coloured flags that fluttered in the sea breeze.

Powerfully built servants of Jagannath wrapped silken ropes around the waists of each of the three deities and raised them, bearing them out from the temple and down the entrance steps along a pathway carpeted with thick cotton pillows. They rocked their huge forms from one pad to the next, and as the heavy deities landed pads burst, sending billows of cotton floating into the air.

In front, as more pads were laid, the pathway was swept by the King using a gold-handled broom, as thousands of onlookers pressed around singing and vibrating all kinds of musical instruments. Sri Chaitanya looked on with loving gaze, calling repeatedly, *'Manima, manima!'*—'Oh Great One!'

Before each chariot was a ramp up which the deities were heaved, until each stood upon their throne high above the throng, attended by servants and priests. When all was ready, beneath a sun already high in the sky, thick ropes were hauled. The chariots rolled slowly and majestically through the broad main street of Jagannath Puri. Watched by the huge crowds on all sides they inched along, sometimes halting, sometimes rolling more quickly, as a hundred thousand adoring devotees sang and danced with drums and musical instruments.

Among his followers moved Mahaprabhu, applying cooling sandalwood paste to their foreheads and giving each one a flower garland. He formed them into seven kirtan groups, each with a lead singer, two drummers and a dancer. Surrounding Jagannath's chariot they began their ecstatic kirtan. At first Mahaprabhu moved from one group to another, then miraculously he was seen to dance in all seven groups at once. Each devotee thought, 'The merciful Lord is dancing in our group alone.' Just as Krishna accompanied each gopi simultaneously in his circle dance of love, so Krishna Chaitanya danced with each of his devotees.

He came in front of Jagannath's chariot, his devotees gathering round him in three circles to protect him from the crowd. As he danced he gazed deep into Jagannath's eyes. He appeared like a spinning circle of flame, calling loudly the names of Krishna and leaping high in the air with tears streaming down his face. Wherever he stepped the earth seemed to tilt. One moment he stood motionless, shivering and pale; then he reddened like a mallika flower, his hairs on end and tears shooting from his eyes like torrents; the next moment, crying and trembling, he fell to the ground and rolled in the white sand. Then Nityananda lifted him gently and held him tight. Such mystical ecstasies had never before been seen.

Among those who witnessed the dancing of Sri Chaitanya before the Rathayatra car, only Svarupa Damodara understood its full significance. He knew his master was expressing the longing felt by Radha to be with Krishna in the forest of Vrindavan. All year long Jagannath lived in his grand temple with the Goddess of Fortune, then for just one week he emerged to be with his devotees among the gardens and lakes around Gundica. Jagannath's journey evoked the occasion when Krishna, as prince of Dvaraka, left his royal city to visit his childhood friends from the forests of Vrindavan. On that occasion Radha came to see her beloved. She had not set eyes upon him since the day at the end of their childhood when Krishna left for the big city, never to return. Since that moment she had spent every waking hour wrapped in thoughts of him, barely able to sustain her life. Now she saw him from a distance and was rendered lifeless. He was a prince with many wives—they could never hope to share again the intimacy of their youth. She longed to be by his side, but knew that could never be. The emotions that filled her heart were the emotions now felt by Mahaprabhu as he danced in front of Jagannath.

'You are the same Krishna who stole my heart during my youth, and I am the same Radha with the same intimate love. We are meeting on the same moonlit night of Chaitra, as the fragrance of malati flowers wafts through the kadamba forest just as in the beginning of our lives. Yet although all this is the same, I long to be with you in the Vrindavan forest, beneath the Vetasi tree on the bank of the Reva.'

'Sei tumi, sei ami, sei nava sangama....'
'You are the same, I am the same, here we meet again.'

So he sang as he danced on and on. It seemed to all who looked that Jagannath upon the chariot watched spellbound as he danced.

While this scene unfolded, the procession reached a wooded garden extending on both sides of the road, appearing just like Vrindavan. This was the place for the lunchtime stop. The chariots halted and thousands of devotees spread among the gardens, laying their cloths upon the ground to prepare lunchtime offerings for Jagannath. Exhausted from his dancing, Sri Chaitanya collapsed beneath the shade of a tree. There on the bare ground he fell into a deep sleep.

NOW WAS THE KING'S CHANCE to come close. He had intently watched Mahaprabhu's dancing, from a distance so as not to disturb him. Encouraged by Sarvabhauma, disguised in the dress of an ordinary devotee, he entered the garden. There he saw Sri Chaitanya lying in the shade with his eyes closed, apparently asleep. Being careful not to disturb him, the King sat at his feet and gently began to massage them.

As he did so he sang softly of the gopis' love for Krishna, chanting Sanskrit verses from the *Bhagavatam*. His gentle voice awoke Mahaprabhu and entranced him. Without opening his eyes he urged the singer to go on, and so came a particular verse sung to Krishna by the gopis.

'Your sweet words, chanted by great souls, give life to those who suffer in this world. The spiritual power of those words spreads everywhere to bless all who hear, dissolving their burden of karma. Those who chant these sweet words offer the most precious gift.'

Mahaprabhu looked to see who was sharing this nectar.

'You yourself are kindest of all,' he exclaimed, 'For you have given me this most wonderful gift.' He repeated the verse again and again, and at length asked the singer's name.

'I am an obedient follower of your devotees,' replied the King. 'Please allow me to remain a servant of your servants.'

If Mahaprabhu recognised the King he did not say. Happily accepting his words he blessed him with a loving embrace and they both wept.

When they saw the King embraced by Mahaprabhu, and at last achieving his personal blessing, all were happy. They knew his good fortune was the result of his persistence and sincere service. That very morning he had personally swept the road in front of Jagannath's chariot.

The King had arranged a wonderful feast, with hundreds of varieties of food liberally distributed. Beggars crowded round and Mahaprabhu took care to see they were all fed, while at the same time asking them to chant the holy names.

'Haribol!' they sang with delight. By the blessings of Chaitanya all were flooded with ecstasy. Happy and full, tired from their exertions, everyone wanted to rest; yet the afternoon was passing and still the procession had some distance to go before reaching its destination, the ancient Gundica temple.

The crowd gathered round the chariot and took up the ropes. But Jagannath's chariot would not move. The King sent his strongest men to pull, and still the chariot stood firm. Elephants were brought from the royal palace and harnessed to the chariot. Crying and bellowing they strained at the ropes but could not advance a single step. An invisible force held the chariot rooted to the ground.

Arriving with his followers, Sri Chaitanya watched the elephants and heard their cries. Ordering the animals released, he brought forward his own devotees and set them to the ropes. With his bare head he pushed the great chariot, and it rolled forward as if it had a life of its own, rattling along without depending on being pulled. All who witnessed this were transfixed. They sang the name of Chaitanya, calling him Gaurachandra, Golden Moon. Ever after, the people remembered this amazing feat—how Chaitanya made Jagannath move when no one else could.

As the afternoon wore on the procession reached its destination, the spotlessly clean Gundica temple. The Jagannath deities were carried inside and once more offered food, with more singing and dancing, then bathed and sung to sleep. Tired and happy, Chaitanya and his followers retired for the night.

For a full week the deities of Jagannath, Balarama and Subhadra remained at Gundica while Chaitanya stayed nearby with his devotees. Sometimes he asked for particular songs to be sung as he danced alone beneath the trees, sometimes he joined them all to dance and sing together. In the gardens surrounding the temple were two lakes, named Indradyumna and Narendra. Diving into their cool waters, with Mahaprabhu in their midst, the devotees splashed and fought like children, reminding some of their childhood games in the Ganges.

Chaitanya immersed himself in the intimate mood of Vrindavan. Among his companions, Svarupa Damodara well understood his feelings. Mahaprabhu asked him to say why the natural beauty of Vrindavan attracted Krishna so.

> 'The land of Vrindavan is made of touchstone and precious crystals. It is a forest of desire trees whose fruits and flowers grant the inhabitants all their wishes. The cows grazing among those trees supply unlimited milk. The water tastes like nectar. The beauty of the cowherd girls surpasses even the beauty of the Goddess of Fortune; their voices are like music, their movements like dancing, their constant companion is the sound of Krishna's flute.'

Srivasa heard Svarupa sing these words and laughed. His devotion belonged to the Goddess of Fortune in Krishna's royal palace, where more reverential feelings for Krishna abounded. He and Svarupa exchanged opinions about their spiritual preferences, and such talks delighted all who heard them. Each devotee had their individual mood of devotion for Krishna—some reverential, some playful, some with heartfelt emotion—each manifesting their own inner spiritual nature.

At the great Jagannath temple the mood was of reverence for Jagannath, Master of the Universe, who lived there in splendour with the Goddess of Fortune. But the time of Rathayatra gave rise to a different mood among many of the devotees. This was the mood of Vrindavan, where Krishna was neither king nor master, but a friend among friends who loved him more than life itself.

Those friends saw him not as Master of the Universe, but as their beloved companion. In his youth Krishna herded cows, played with his friends and danced at night in the groves with the young girls. He was neither king nor master. The forest people thought of him not as God, but as their friend, their child, their lover. They worshipped him without hope of something in return; they gave only the uncondi- tional love that is the characteristic of Vrindavan.

Jagannath in his majestic temple never forgot those loving exchanges of his youth and always longed to be back among those companions immersed in pure love, uninhibited by reverence. Each year at Rathayatra, leaving behind his queens and royal palaces, the Lord of the Universe took with him his brother Balarama and sister Subhadra to seek out the intimate company of his childhood friends. This Vrindavan feeling was the mood that pervaded Chaitanya's whole life and made Rathayatra so special to him.

On the ninth day festivities drew to a close. A great procession followed the deities on their chariots back to the main temple of Jagannath Puri. So the magical week in Vrindavan passed and Jagannath with his servants returned to his palace for another year.

THE TIME CAME FOR the devotees from Bengal to return home. Before they left, Mahaprabhu called them together for special words of guidance. First he took aside his faithful brother Nityananda. Though they were not related by birth, he always looked upon Nityananda as his elder brother, while Nityananda, though fourteen years the senior, thought of Mahaprabhu as his master—indeed he dedicated his life to inspiring others to give his Lord their love and devotion,

'Brother, I need you to stay in Bengal to lead my mission,' Mahaprabhu told him. 'I see no one else who can succeed at this difficult task. Take with you some trusted helpers, and give everyone the gift of devotion for Krishna.' Following this order Nityananda became the charismatic leader of the devotees in Bengal, tirelessly travelling about the country to spread love of God.

Then Mahaprabhu addressed Advaita. He asked him to teach Krishna devotion among the less fortunate people. Too often those outside the higher castes were ignored by the brahmin teachers and left to fend for themselves. Advaita had always felt a special concern for the welfare of these people. Mahaprabhu therefore relied on him to give them the same chance as others to enter the path of Krishna consciousness.

One by one, he said farewell to the devotees, giving each one personal words of encouragement. Inspired by his instructions they prepared to set off on their journey, contemplating how they would help Nityananda fulfil the mission he had been given.

As they were about to leave, one of them asked Mahaprabhu how a householder should practice spiritual life.

'Always chant the name of Krishna, and serve the Vaishnavas,' he answered, speaking to them all.

'How can we recognise a true Vaishnava?' they asked.

'Whoever ceaselessly chants Krishna's name should be honoured as the best of persons. No other spiritual practice is necessary, for Krishna's name dissolves all obstacles on the spiritual path. His name not only frees a soul from material conditioning, but also awakens the soul's natural love for Krishna. Therefore one who chants Krishna's name is a true Vaishnava.'

As he bade farewell he left these final words:

> 'And among Vaishnavas, one whose mere presence inspires others to chant Krishna's name is dearest of all.'

The one most dear

ONCE NITYANANDA returned to Bengal he abandoned his former austere ways and went through an unexpected transformation. He took to wearing brightly coloured clothes with multi-coloured silk turbans, long flower garlands, necklaces of pearls, earrings, bracelets, and rings of gold upon each of his fingers. He gathered around him young followers, also brightly dressed, expert singers, dancers and musicians who went with him, their singing and dancing enchanting the people. Among his following were many boys whom he cared for like his own sons. With Nityananda as their leader they played together spreading joy wherever they went. Since Chaitanya's move to Puri people had become unhappy, for they had lost their dearest companion. Now, inspired by Nityananda, they forgot their cares and came back to life.

He came to Saci's house. She had never recovered from the loss of her son, but now she found new hope, feeling his presence in the form of his eternal brother, Nityananda. She begged him to stay nearby and Nityananda agreed. He made Navadvipa his headquarters, and from there he travelled Bengal to spread Mahaprabhu's sankirtan movement.

So it was that although Chaitanya now lived in Puri, his movement continued to grow in Bengal by the mercy of Nityananda. He showed special concern toward the ones who had fallen to the bottom of society, the very poorest who struggled to feed themselves, the outcasts, even the criminals; all were touched by his open-hearted friendship and generous spirit. Anyone who had escaped Nimai's touch was now captured by Nitai. Navadvipa became like a royal city where vagabonds and thieves reformed and became devotees of Krishna.

One of Nityananda's followers, named Gadadhara Das, approached the local Muslim overlord, who was ferocious in his opposition to their chanting. Gadadhara fearlessly begged him to chant the name of Hari, but the Kazi was dismissive.

'Go home, Gadadhara. Tomorrow I will chant Hari.' Gadadhara clapped his hands with joy.

'Now you have chanted the name Hari, and your sins have vanished,' he cried.

In such ways, Muslims were influenced to chant Krishna's names and the spirit of the sankirtan movement spread more and more, thanks to Nityananda and his band of chanting devotees.

10

LOOKING FOR KRISHNA

IN PURI FOUR YEARS PASSED. Each summer devotees from Bengal visited their beloved Nimai and joined him to celebrate Rathayatra. Mahaprabhu was happy in Puri, but his mind dwelt on going to Krishna's homeland. Ever since receiving Krishna's name from his guru in Gaya he had longed to go to Vrindavan, but there had been interruptions.

First he had returned to his family and established the path of devotion to Krishna among his own people in Navadvipa; then when he became a sannyasi, to please his mother he had moved to Jagannath Puri instead of Vrindavan; and travelled and preached in South India, as a sannyasi should. Now the journey to Vrindavan was ever in his thoughts.

When Rathayatra was completed Mahaprabhu told his companions it was time for him to go on pilgrimage to Krishna's sacred land. Previously when he had mentioned this they had not wanted him to go, partly because the journey was hazardous, and partly because they were afraid of losing him. This time however, they gave way.

'If you must go, wait for the rains to end when the roads are easier to travel.'

So it was agreed. Three months later, on Vijaya Dasami, the day commemorating Rama's victory over Ravana and marking the change of season, Mahaprabhu set out. He planned to travel north along the coast as far as Bengal, where he would visit his mother and bathe in the Ganges at Navadvipa, then to follow the course of the Ganges and Yamuna Rivers until he reached Vrindavan.

He set out with a large company of devotees. The first part of his journey brought him to Bhubaneswar, capital city of Orissa, full of ornate temples. Here he was met by King Prataparudra. The King made elaborate arrangements for his onward journey, ordering rest houses to be prepared at stopping places along the way, and assigning a bodyguard to travel with him. Where he was to cross the great River Mahanadi, the King ordered the spot to be marked for posterity.

'I will go there to bathe, and may I also die there,' he declared.

Accompanied by his queens, the King gave Mahaprabhu a royal send-off, and in easy stages the party reached the northern borders of Orissa, where the Bay of Bengal meets the mouth of the Ganges. This marked the limit of the King's authority, and his officers and bodyguards prepared to say farewell. Beyond lay country patrolled by guards loyal to Nawab Husain Shah, the Muslim ruler of Bengal. The Nawab was at war with Orissa and had already destroyed many Hindu temples. To guarantee Mahaprabhu's safe onward passage, the King's officers negotiated with their Muslim counterparts. For a few days messages passed back and forth, then to everyone's surprise Husain Shah himself arrived to see Mahaprabhu. The Nawab's curiosity had been aroused by reports that had reached him, and when he met Sri Chaitanya in person he was genuinely moved by his spirituality. The pious Muslim offered his personal help, lending boats and guards to take the party into the waters of the Ganges delta.

When they embarked, Gadadhara wanted to come with them. He had insisted on being part of the group even though Mahaprabhu had asked him to stay in Puri. Now he was told he could come no further. Gadadhara could not bear to be separated from the one who was his life and soul.

'Dear Gadadhara, your service to Krishna lies in Puri, and that is where you belong—I will soon return to you.'

Gadadhara ignored these entreaties but now Mahaprabhu was firm. Gadadhara's eyes filled with tears as he watched the boats move swiftly into the stream while Mahaprabhu looked steadfastly away. Gadadhara fell to the ground distraught, and was comforted by the small group of friends who helped him recover and took him with them back to Puri.

Mahaprabhu and his party were carried safely into the mouth of the Ganges, protected by the Nawab's guards from the pirates who haunted those waters. Journeying along wide palm-thronged channels, they passed upstream deep into Bengal, as far as Panihati, a safe journey from the district of Nadia.

So it was that four years after his departure as a lone sannyasi, Sri Krishna Chaitanya re-entered his homeland, with a government escort, to the joy and surprise of his Bengal devotees.

For three weeks he moved from house to house, staying with Srivasa, Sivananda Sena and Vidya Vacaspati the brother of Sarvabhauma. Word of his presence spread, and wherever he went he was besieged by crowds of eager devotees. At Vidya Vacaspati's home near Navadvipa, the crowds overran the surrounding countryside. So many tried to cross the Ganges to see him that the river became thick with people, desperate for a glimpse of him. Some of the overladen boats capsized, though no one perished. Seeing these vast numbers and not wanting to endanger people's lives, Mahaprabhu slipped away in the night to another part of Navadvipa. When dawn came and people discovered he had left, they searched for him and soon found him at another house. Again they gathered in their thousands. This time he showed himself to the crowds, and the air resounded with the sound of Krishna's names. Seeing their vast numbers and hearing their thunderous kirtan he wept with joy. He and Nityananda joined with them, dancing in ecstasy. All who witnessed these events felt themselves floating in an ocean of bliss, and were freed forever from the bonds of birth and death.

Eventually he reached Advaita Acarya's house in Shantipur, where his mother was able to be with him and gain some relief from her years of separation. He stayed for some days, then set off on the road to Vrindavan.

He was travelling amid a great company of followers, and as they passed through fields and villages, more and more came to join them. With Mahaprabhu were Haridas and the others who had started out with him from Puri. They were joined by many more from Navadvipa, led by Nityananda, Srivasa, Mukunda and Murari. All were intent on staying with him all the way to Vrindavan. The party followed the main roads from village to village near the Ganges, their numbers growing ever larger. As they passed through the countryside, huge crowds flocked to see him. Wherever he trod they took handfuls of dust from the ground, leaving holes in the road. In this way he reached the village of Ramakeli, which stood by the banks of the Ganges close to Gauda, capital of Bengal.

Here lived two gifted brothers who had risen to become youthful ministers in the government of Nawab Husain Shah. They came from a high-caste brahmin family originating in South India, but had adopted the Muslim titles Sakar Mallik and Dabir Khas in the service of the government. Their learning and sharp intelligence, and the high esteem in which they were held, made them much valued by the Nawab. Despite their youth—they were still in their twenties—the ruler had made them among his closest and most trusted advisers, appointing one his Private

Secretary and the other his Treasurer. Privately, however, they were devotees of Krishna, and for some time had been sending secret letters to Mahaprabhu professing their devotion to him.

In the night, hidden from prying eyes, the two brothers came to see him. They bowed full length on the ground and tearfully offered him prayers.

'We feel ashamed to come before you, because we are sinful. But you are the saviour of Jagai and Madhai, come to save fallen people like us. Other than you, who can rescue us from our degraded condition? Though we are like dwarves who want to catch the moon, we aspire for your mercy. Please allow us to serve you.'

Mahaprabhu heard their humble words and was moved to tears.

'Please arise and don't speak like this,' he implored. 'I know your hearts are full of love for Krishna, for I have read your letters. Did you not receive my reply? I wrote that a woman with a secret lover may appear busy serving her husband, but in her heart she thinks always of her lover. You should be the same.' So saying he laid his hands on their heads.

'People may wonder why I came here. They do not know it was just to see you two. I give you the names Rupa and Sanatan. You are my eternal servants and have been so through many births. Do not fear, Krishna will soon release you from your entanglement.' He then embraced them.

The two brothers had to hurry away, but before leaving Sanatan had some advice for Mahaprabhu. He was attracting unwelcome attention, Sanatan said, particularly from Husain Shah and his Muslim deputies. The Nawab had offered him protection while in his kingdom, but Sanatan feared that when he saw the size of the crowds who followed Mahaprabhu he might change his mind. Sanatan's advice was not to travel so conspicuously. In his opinion it would be better if he went to Vrindavan alone, without drawing attention to himself.

On hearing Sanatan's advice Mahaprabhu decided he must abandon his journey to Vrindavan. Instead he would return to Jagannath Puri and later make a separate pilgrimage. So, having reached Ramakeli and blessed Rupa and Sanatan, he returned the way he had come, again staying at Advaita's home in Bengal.

ON THIS RETURN JOURNEY one exceptional young man came to see Mahaprabhu. This was Raghunath, whose father was a wealthy benefactor of the Vaishnavas and close friend of Advaita's. Four years earlier, when Sri Krishna Chaitanya had stayed at Advaita's house as a new sannyasi, the youthful Raghunath had been allowed to serve him, and Sri Chaitanya had placed his feet on Raghunath's head. The youth had been so affected that he wanted to leave everything at once and accompany Chaitanya to Jagannath Puri, but his father had forbidden him. Since then he had stayed at home thinking only of how he could renounce his family and join Sri

Chaitanya in Puri. His father had other ideas; he wanted his son to settle down and help look after the family's extensive landholdings: he arranged a match for him with a beautiful young wife and did everything he could to keep him comfortably at home. At the same time he took the precaution of setting men to watch his son day and night. Raghunath felt trapped.

Now he heard that Mahaprabhu was again staying with Advaita, and begged his father's leave to go there. Reluctantly his father agreed, sending a party of servants to watch over Raghunath, and making him promise to return within a week. So it was that Raghunath came to Shantipur. When Mahaprabhu saw him he knew the young man's mind was full of thoughts of running away to Jagannath Puri. He spoke lovingly but firmly.

'Krishna will soon deliver you from the ocean of material life,' he told Raghunath. 'But until then you should return home and live normally. Enjoy what Krishna has given you, without allowing yourself to become attached. When the time is right, in a year or two, and I have completed my pilgrimage to Vrindavan, you can join me in Puri. Krishna will show you how.'

Encouraged by these words Raghunath returned home with a peaceful heart. His parents saw the change in him and relaxed their guard. So he lived at home a while longer, behaving as a responsible householder and patiently waiting for Krishna to release him.

For seven days Mahaprabhu stayed with Advaita while his mother cooked for him. This was the last time mother and son were together in this life, and their eventual parting was full of sorrow.

Quietly taking his leave, Mahaprabhu journeyed back to Puri with only a few companions. He had been away for eight months, given his love to countless thousands, initiated two young men destined to do great things, and encouraged Raghunath. But he had failed to reach Vrindavan. Once back in Puri he resumed preparations for his pilgrimage.

ON RETURNING FROM HIS TRAVELS, Mahaprabhu told his friends of the crowds he had encountered previously.

'So many thousands pressed around me it was difficult to move.' He took Gadadhara's hand. 'Dear friend, Krishna was unhappy when I left you behind. That's why he stopped me going.'

Although he had not reached Vrindavan, he had met Rupa and Sanatan, and in some ways that had been the real purpose of his journey. He told his companions about these two young men whose learning and humility had made such a deep impression upon him.

'Their advice was good. They said I should travel alone to Vrindavan. That is how Madhavendra Puri went there, and I shall do the same. My dear friends, you must let me do this.'

So it was settled. He would stay in Puri for the rainy season, then leave for Vrindavan with just two companions: a quiet and capable brahmin named Balabhadra Bhattacarya who was a scholar and a cook, and an assistant named Krishnadas.

Four months later, at the end of the rainy season, unseen by prying eyes, Mahaprabhu slipped away from Puri. In the half-light before dawn he and his two companions disappeared into the jungle. Their path led them away from the main road to escape notice, entering wild places where no humans venture. As they passed deep into the jungle they saw elephants, tigers, boars and rhinoceros. Mahaprabhu's companions were afraid, but he quietly chanted Krishna's names, counting on his fingers. Under his spell the animals moved aside without harming them. One day a tiger lay in their path and Mahaprabhu touched it with his foot. Springing to its feet, the tiger began to dance and call the name of Krishna. Another time they reached a riverbank where Mahaprabhu sat to meditate. A herd of elephants came out of the forest and stood silently staring at him. Suddenly he splashed them playfully and commanded, 'Chant Krishna!' The elephants swayed their ponderous heads with pleasure, trumpeting Krishna's names.

As he walked, constantly chanting, Mahaprabhu's sweet voice attracted deer, who noiselessly followed him. Overhead flew peacocks, also calling Krishna's names. In his presence animals who were natural enemies became friends, and the weak no longer feared the strong. All creatures felt his love and danced together joyfully.

Wild roots and vegetables were plentiful in the forest; in the villages along the way people gave them rice, and Balabhadra was expert at collecting ingredients for their meals. Mahaprabhu taught the villagers to chant the holy name. Whoever heard him chant taught a second, who taught a third. So the chanting spread as he walked through the forest in great happiness, chanting Krishna's names and thinking of Vrindavan. After a month they had crossed the range of hills bordering north-east Orissa and reached their halfway point, Varanasi on the banks of the Ganges. This was North India's principal centre of pilgrimage and learning.

Here waited the pious Tapana Misra. Ten years earlier he had met Chaitanya, then the young householder Nimai Pandit, touring and teaching in East Bengal. At that time Chaitanya had ordered him to go and settle in Varanasi, promising that one day they would meet again. Since then Tapana Misra had lived here with his family, patiently waiting for his master's word to be fulfilled. One morning he came to the Ganges to bathe and saw the same Sri Chaitanya beside the water's edge. With a cry he ran forward to catch his master's feet. They embraced and Tapana Misra brought him to his house, where he fed him and made him comfortable. Then he hurried off to find his friend Chandrasekhar. They both held deep faith for Krishna, though they found few others to share it with in this city of learning, where the main topic of discussion was the philosophy of oneness, *advaita*, and where personal devotion to Krishna was looked upon as sentiment for those who had not come to the higher stage of realising their oneness with God.

The most respected teacher of Varanasi was the sannyasi Prakasananda Sarasvati. He had heard from friends in Puri of the young sannyasi named Sri Krishna Chaitanya, but held no great regard for him. In his opinion a sannyasi's duty was to study scripture, not to spend his time singing and dancing, and gathering sentimental followers. When he heard that this same Krishna Chaitanya was in Varanasi, Prakasananda laughed aloud.

Tapana Misra and Chandrasekhar were troubled by this ridicule from Prakasananda, and hurried to tell Mahaprabhu, who simply smiled. For now he was intent on going to Vrindavan. On his way back, he said, he would meet this proud Prakasananda and his followers.

For ten days Sri Chaitanya stayed at Tapana Misra's home. Then he continued on his way. Reaching the confluence of the Ganges and Yamuna at Prayag, he stayed for three days to bathe in those holy waters. From there he joined the River Yamuna, so dear to Krishna, and his ecstasy deepened. Following the path along her banks he encountered many along the way and taught them to chant Krishna's names. Wherever he went he spread his message of love for God.

They came at last to Mathura, birthplace of Krishna, where they met a brahmin disciple of Madhavendra Puri. Though his name was not widely known, Madhavendra had been a learned and surrendered soul who initiated his followers into the innermost secrets of *madhurya rasa*, the loving affairs of Radha and Krishna. Madhavendra's disciples included Advaita Acarya, Nityananda, and Mahaprabhu's own guru, Isvara Puri. Consquently Mahaprabhu revered Madhavendra Puri as his grand-preceptor and a uniquely important teacher. He felt blessed to meet a disciple of this great Vaishnava, and when the brahmin invited Mahaprabhu to stay in his home he gladly accepted. He stayed there in Mathura and visited Krishna's birthplace beneath Kamsa's palace, then he entered the land of Vrindavan.

SRI CHAITANYA BEGAN HIS PILGRIMAGE through the twelve sacred forests. The land was remote and sparsely populated, filled with abundant wildlife. Entering this paradise, he was transported to another world. Cows came up and licked him, deer heard his sweet voice and flocked around him; parrots, cuckoos and bees hovered about his head; trees and creepers blossomed in his presence and lowered their branches, fruit-laden, to touch his feet. The whole forest came alive, as if all living things recognised their Lord Krishna, returned to be among them.

Whatever ecstasy Mahaprabhu had shown in Puri here increased many times as he wandered among the trees and creatures of Vrindavan. He embraced the deer and constantly chanted 'Krishna, Krishna'. The sight of the blue-throated peacocks made him faint, for in the cries of the peacocks and the chirping of the green parrots he heard the names of Radha and Krishna.

He came to sacred Govardhana Hill, once lifted by Krishna's hand. Beside the hill were the two ponds of Radha and Shyama. These were to him the most sacred places on Earth, where Radha and Krishna used to meet and bathe. But now people no longer knew what they were. Mahaprabhu recognised them and re-established them as sacred ponds where pilgrims could come to bathe and offer prayers to Radha and Krishna.

He stayed in the shelter of Govardhana Hill for many days. Seeing the hill's beauty he sang a verse from the *Srimad Bhagavatam*:

> 'Govardhana Hill is the dearest servant of the Lord!
> Touched by His lotus feet it joyfully gives fresh water,
> soft grass, edible roots, vegetables and sheltering caves
> to serve Krishna and Balarama with their friends
> and cows.'

He continued through each of the forests until he came to the original Vrindavan forest on the banks of the Yamuna River, the very place where Krishna danced with the gopis. Here Sri Chaitanya stayed for several weeks, as autumn turned to winter and the Yamuna's waters grew cold and misty. He sat in the pale morning sun beneath an old tamarind tree, chanting Krishna's names as he gazed at the Yamuna. This place was called Amlitala, the place of the tamarind tree. In the afternoon people would gather around him, and he taught them to chant.

As word of the devout young sannyasi spread, more and more flocked to see him. Crowds grew, and Balabhadra Bhattacarya, who had faithfully cared for Mahaprabhu ever since they left Puri, found the numbers becoming oppressive for his master. He reasoned that Mahaprabhu had done what he set out to do: he had seen Vrindavan and visited the holy places more or less alone and undisturbed. Now the longer he stayed the more he would attract unwelcome attention. So Balabhadra decided it was time for them to leave Vrindavan and return to Puri.

Quietly one morning, in the short days of winter, Mahaprabhu left Krishna's land. Travelling in a small party of four, he retraced his steps, following the path by the Yamuna.

ONE DAY CAME AN UNUSUAL MEETING beside the river. They reached a shady spot where Sri Chaitanya paused to give his four companions a chance to rest. In the distance he could hear the sound of a young cowherd playing his flute, and as he listened he fell into a trance and stopped breathing.

A company of ten mounted soldiers approached and halted, eyeing the group with suspicion. They were members of the Pathan military order, and were led by the King's son

Vijuli Khan. Seeing an unconscious sannyasi lying on the ground, surrounded by four travellers, they suspected foul play.

'You rogues have poisoned this sannyasi and stolen his gold,' they declared. 'We will arrest you and put you to death.'

The brahmin Balabhadra, unafraid, was the first to speak.

'This sannyasi is my guru. Sometimes he falls unconscious like this. Wait with us and soon he will awaken. Then you can ask him anything you like.'

Still the soldiers distrusted them.

'You are all rogues,' they repeated.

Among the four travellers was Krishnadas. Being of Rajput descent he stood tall and fearless.

'I am a Rajput,' he declared. 'Nearby I have stationed two hundred Turkish soldiers and a hundred cannon. If you threaten us I will summon them. They will kill you and take your horses.'

The Pathans hesitated. Just then Mahaprabhu awoke. Loudly calling the name of Krishna, he raised his arms and began dancing. The Muslims were shaken and their hearts were seized with fear. Some of them bowed to Mahaprabhu.

Among them was a man dressed in black, whom they revered as their teacher. He came before Sri Chaitanya to expound monist philosophy, quoting from the Qur'an to describe God as the all-pervading impersonal spirit. Sri Chaitanya heard what he had to say, then responded.

'The Qur'an teaches of pious deeds, mystic philosophy, meditation and the impersonal brahman,' replied Mahaprabhu.

'But ultimately the Qur'an concludes there is one God, an eternal divine person whose form is blackish, who should be served in devotion. He is the Absolute Truth, the all-pervading, omniscient eternal being, origin of all. Creation, maintenance and dissolution come from Him. He is the cause of all causes and shelter of all beings. By service to God in devotion the living entity is freed from material existence. Love at His lotus feet is the ultimate goal of life. The happiness of merging into God's existence cannot be compared to even a fragment of the transcendental bliss that comes from service to God's lotus feet.'

The Muslim teacher listened in rapt attention.

'The Qur'an ultimately establishes the Lord's personal feature as the highest truth,' concluded Mahaprabhu. 'You know the Qur'an: what is your conclusion?'

'I accept all you say,' the scholar replied. 'Now I have seen you and heard you chant the name of Krishna, and have myself sung Krishna's name, my pride in being a scholar has gone. I surrender to you.'

Saying this the man in black fell at Chaitanya's feet and begged him to teach him the ultimate goal of life.

'Please get up,' said Mahaprabhu. 'You have chanted Krishna's holy name so your sins from millions of lifetimes are gone. Now you are pure.' Then he turned to all the Pathans and commanded them.

'Sing the name of Krishna! Sing the name of Krishna!'

They sang Krishna's name and were overwhelmed in ecstasy. Their teacher was initiated by Mahaprabhu with the name Ramadas, servant of Rama. Their leader, the King's son Vijuli Khan, also surrendered to Sri Chaitanya, who placed his foot on the young man's head.

After meeting Mahaprabhu these men's lives were transformed. They gave up their possessions and became mendicants. Wherever they went they glorified Sri Chaitanya. They became known as the Pathan Vaishnavas, and their leader Vijuli Khan was celebrated at holy places as a great teacher.

Sri Chaitanya and his companions continued to walk along the Yamuna, following the river in the direction of Prayag and Varanasi.

Chaitanya had achieved his life's ambition to visit Krishna's home, but before returning to Puri he still had important work to accomplish.

Book Three

HEART

11

ETERNAL TEACHINGS

AFTER THEIR NIGHT-TIME TALKS in Ramakeli the two brothers Rupa and Sanatan had returned back to their official duties. The experience of meeting Sri Krishna Chaitanya face to face was profound. Their hearts had been opened and bound them to him with deep love. Now they knew the purpose of their lives: they would dedicate themselves to his service, and to do this they must extricate themselves from their burdens of government. Enough of their lives had been given over to mundane affairs and they both felt it was time for radical change. Sanatan began staying at home where he surrounded himself with learned scholars of Vaishnava scripture. He sent word to the court that he was unwell, and simply immersed himself in hearing and studying the great holy book of Vaishnaivism, *Srimad Bhagavatam*—as had been his favourite occupation in his childhood.

However, he was wary of how his master Nawab Husain Shah, feared ruler of Bengal, would respond to his absence. Sanatan was his chief minister and the Nawab depended on him to run affairs while he was away on his endless military campaigns. One day without warning the ruler appeared on Sanatan's doorstep, demanding to know where he had been all this time. When he heard that Sanatan wanted to retire he was outraged. He felt some affection for Sanatan, treating him almost like a younger brother, but if he was crossed his mood could quickly change. He placed Sanatan under house arrest, watched over by an armed guard. Saying he would decide what to do with him when he returned, he left on another of his never-ending fighting expeditions.

While Sanatan was confined to his home studying the sacred texts, Rupa learned that Mahaprabhu had set off on his pilgrimage to Krishna's holy land. Rupa quickly concluded his affairs in the hope of meeting Mahaprabhu in Vrindavan. Before leaving Bengal he deposited ten thousand gold coins with a trusted local merchant, and a message for Sanatan to use the money to escape and join him in Vrindavan. With all arrangements made Rupa set off with his younger brother Anupama. Their path led them by the Ganges as far as Prayag, from where they would follow the Yamuna to Vrindavan.

MAHAPRABHU THOUGHT OF RUPA AND SANATAN. Early in the year 1516 he was walking along the path by the Yamuna back toward Bengal, approaching Prayag from the opposite direction. From the moment he had met the two brothers he knew they were the ones he would teach. With their intelligence and learning, their worldly abilities, their deep knowledge of the *Bhagavatam* nurtured since childhood, but most of all their pure-hearted devotion, they would understand him and know how to pass on his teachings to succeeding generations.

Accompanied by his two assistants Mahaprabhu again reached the confluence of the Ganges and the Yamuna at Prayag, and halted there to bathe during the great winter festival of Magh Mela. With perfect timing, beside the temple of Madhava, he met Rupa and his younger brother Anupama. From a distance they saw one another. The two brothers bowed low with humility, and their effulgent Lord, glowing amid an adoring crowd, hastened over to embrace them.

Rupa had composed a Sanskrit prayer specially for this moment, and now he offered it.

> *namo maha-vadanyaya*
> *krishna-prema-pradaya te*
> *krishnaya krishna-caitanya*
> *namne gaura-tvishe namaha*

'I bow to the kindest one of all. You give pure love for Krishna. You are Krishna by the name Krishna Chaitanya. I bow before your golden form.'

Mahaprabhu embraced the two brothers with great happiness, telling them Krishna had freed them forever from the prison of material life. Now he would teach Rupa the secrets of Krishna consciousness. A few days passed, then at the Dasasvamedha bathing ghat on the edge of town they sat together for ten days.

Sri Chaitanya taught Rupa the truth about Krishna, about service to Krishna, and about the intimate secrets of love between Krishna and the ones who loved him. He began by describing the truth about Krishna and his creation.

THE OCEAN OF LOVE

'THE OCEAN OF DEVOTION is so vast no one can estimate where it begins or ends. I will describe to you just one drop.

'This universe contains numberless living beings, all tiny sparks of the Supreme Spirit. They migrate from one species to another, from one planet to another, in a cycle of birth and death that has continued since time immemorial. Some live as immobile entities such as plants or stones; others move in the sea, in the air or over the land. Among those who move on the land, humans are few, and civilized humans fewer still. Of all these, the ones who have no desire other than to serve Krishna are most rare.

'These compassionate devotees of Krishna live in this world only to enlighten lost souls and pass on the seed of love for Krishna. If by the mercy of such a servant of Krishna one receives the seed of devotion one must sow it in the garden of the heart. Water that seed by chanting Krishna's names, or by speaking and hearing of Krishna with Krishna's devotees. The seed will grow into the creeper of devotion. Continue to water that creeper and it will climb beyond this universe to enter the effulgence of the spiritual sky, where gradually it will reach the planet of Goloka Vrindavan. There it will embrace the desire tree of Krishna's lotus feet and put forth fruits of divine love.

'The gardener must continue watering the plant and beware of the great enemy of devotion—to harbour envy toward a compassionate servant of Krishna. If you hold onto such feelings you invite a mad elephant into the garden of the heart, that will trample the creeper of devotion and risk destroying everything. Regular chanting of Krishna's name with faith and humility nourishes the creeper of devotion and protects it from this danger.

'When chanting the Lord's names one must be careful to avoid certain pitfalls. The greatest mistake is to criticise the ones who are dedicated to teaching about Krishna. Other errors are to imagine that Krishna's name is not the same as Krishna Himself; to think one's spiritual master an ordinary person; to think that Krishna's name is equalled by any other name one may chant; to continue sinful life in the belief that chanting will counteract your sins; or to glorify Krishna's name among the faithless. Above all when chanting, give up your material attachments and replace them with attachment to Krishna.

'Other obstacles are greed, pride, violence toward other living beings, desire for material comfort, fame and followers, and the lure of mystic powers. These weeds can flourish alongside the sacred creeper of devotion—they must be sought out and cut away. All these material desires prevent the appearance of pure devotion. The final illusion of this world is the wish to become God.

'A devotee wants only service at the feet of Krishna, which fulfils all desires. The soul who enters the path of constant service to Krishna becomes attached to Him alone, leaving aside all other forms of God to focus on Krishna and on the sound of Krishna's name. The mind of this devoted one, upon hearing the glories and qualities of Krishna, flows toward the Lord as the Ganges flows to the sea.

'Devotion begins by hearing with faith from a devotee of Krishna. In the company of devotees one learns the ways of devotional service beginning with hearing, chanting and remembering. As you become absorbed in these services you are freed from doubts, the impurities in your heart are washed away, and firm faith is established. When faith is firm there arises an increasing taste for Krishna, then deep attachment, then continuous ecstasy, and eventually *prema*—pure love of God. As sugarcane juice is refined into molasses, then sugar, then solid crystals, so this love increases over time to become continuous ecstatic love for the Lord.

'Attachment for Krishna has five primary tastes called *rasa*. They are named *santa, dasya, sakhya, vatsalya* and *madhurya*. These are: passive adoration of Krishna's greatness; dependence on Krishna in the mood of service; love for Krishna in friendship; love for Krishna as one's child; and love for Krishna as lover and beloved.

'When passive adoration of Krishna's greatness increases in reverence it grows into service; when service becomes more intimate it manifests friend-ship, in which the sense of reverence is replaced by a feeling of equality; as friendship increases in affec-tion and caring for the Lord it becomes parental love, in which Krishna depends on the devotee's care; and when all these feelings grow in intimacy and intensity conjugal love arises, which includes all the other *rasas*.

Just as the qualities of ether, air, fire and water are all included in earth, so conjugal love is the culmination of all relationships.

'Always think of Krishna and He will manifest in your heart. So you will reach the shore of the ocean of transcendental love.'

FOR TEN DAYS Mahaprabhu sat with Rupa beside the River Ganges teaching him everything about pure love for Krishna. He asked Rupa to write down all he had heard, and to describe the secrets of *bhaktirasa*, the deep and varied emotions of the soul to serve Krishna. Then he embraced Rupa and told him to go to Vrindavan. Rupa wanted to go with his master to Jagannath Puri, but now was not to be the time. Mahaprabhu said that later Rupa could come and visit him in Puri—first he must go on to Vrindavan.

Sri Chaitanya boarded a boat while Rupa watched from the shore as his master slipped downstream toward Varanasi. In intense grief Rupa fainted and had to be helped to his lodgings. The next day he and Anupama left for Vrindavan.

Mahaprabhu did not look back. As his boat glided away his thoughts were on Rupa's brother Sanatan, for whom he had a special mission, and on the philosopher monks of Varanasi. Soon he would meet them all, win their trust and speak to them about Krishna.

A few days later he arrived at Varanasi, where he was met outside the town by his loyal servants Chandrasekhar and Tapana Misra. They led him and his attendants to their homes. Mahaprabhu stayed with Chandrasekhar, and his attendants became guests of Tapana Misra.

SANATAN HAD BEEN under house arrest in Bengal. But the trusted merchant had managed to deliver Rupa's message and gold coins. Sanatan lost no time in buying his freedom with seven thousand coins, advising the head guard to say he had drowned himself in the Ganges.

'Have no fear,' he assured the guard. 'I will not be seen here again: I will retire from the world and travel to Mecca.' Which was more or less the truth, for as soon as Sanatan had been helped across the river he disappeared into the hills and travelled west by wild country tracks in the direction of Varanasi. Passers-by saw only a poor mendicant dressed in torn clothes and carrying no possessions. It was winter and the nights were cold, but Sanatan was happy and free from cares, intent upon giving his life to the service of Sri Chaitanya Mahaprabhu. On the road he happened to meet his wealthy brother-in-law Srikanta, who promised secrecy and gave him a fine woollen shawl to keep him warm.

After several weeks on the road Sanatan arrived in Varanasi at the same time that Mahaprabhu himself was there. Hearing of his Lord's presence, he made his way to the house where he was staying. There he sat on the ground outside and waited patiently.

INSIDE THE HOUSE Mahaprabhu spoke to his host.

'Go outside and see if there is a Vaishnava at your door.'

Chandrasekhar went out and looked in front of his house. He saw no sign of Sanatan, only a bearded Muslim mendicant sitting nearby. Returning, he reported to Mahaprabhu that no Vaishnava was there.

'Look again, and whoever is there bring him in,' ordered Mahaprabhu. So Chandrasekhar called the mendicant into his courtyard. Mahaprabhu at once recognised Sanatan and ran to embrace him. Reunited, the two held each other and wept with deep emotion. Then Sanatan remembered himself and pulled away.

'Please do not hold me, Lord, I am not worthy of your touch.'

'On the contrary,' replied Mahaprabhu, 'I am purified by touching you. Because you always remember Krishna you are yourself a holy shrine. Just to see you, touch you or speak of you is my perfection. Believe me, those whom the world honours but who do not serve Krishna are not so good as the least of those devoted to Krishna. So the scriptures tell us.'

Mahaprabhu led Sanatan inside and gave him a seat, then asked about his escape from the Nawab. After hearing his story he sent him with Chandrasekhar to get cleaned up and dressed in fresh clothes. Sanatan accepted only simple cloth, not the fine robes Chandrasekhar offered him. He wanted to give up unnecessary comforts. He found a poor pilgrim and gave him his finely-woven woollen shawl in exchange for the pilgrim's old worn cloth.

When Mahaprabhu saw that Sanatan had given away his last remaining comfort he felt even more love for him. Now he was ready to teach Sanatan everything about Krishna, about the art of service to Krishna, and about the highest stages of divine love. Sanatan submitted himself before his master.

'I have fallen into the well of material enjoyment. People may have thought me wise, but I know nothing. Now you have rescued me, please tell me what I should do, who I am, why I suffer in this world, and how I can be healed. Be merciful and show me the truth.'

Being so asked, Mahaprabhu revealed his confidential teachings to Sanatan. One after another he covered three topics: 1) the soul and its relationship with Krishna; 2) how to revive that eternal relationship; and 3) the ultimate goal of life. He began with the soul.

THE PATH OF DEVOTION

1

'THE INNERMOST NATURE of the soul is to be the eternal servant of Krishna. Krishna's potencies are three: spirit, matter and soul. The innumerable souls belong to the realm of spirit, but some freely choose to enter the realm of matter. Those souls who choose to turn away from Krishna enter these worlds of matter and become enveloped by fear and illusion. The way for them to find release from this fear is to seek Krishna's shelter. Krishna has the power to dispel the illusion, for He creates it. In his mercy Krishna guides these souls through holy books and teachers. He reminds them of their eternal relationship with God. Ultimately He guides them to discover God as the Supreme Person, Krishna.

'Now I will speak about the soul's relationship with Krishna.

'Krishna lives everywhere in his creation. Whatever you experience comes from Krishna. He expands into innumerable divine forms, each equivalent to his original form of Godhead—just as innumerable candles lit from one original candle are each equal in power to that original candle. These multiple forms of God pervade reality and stand guardian in all directions at all times—as protector, father, mother and friend. They are described in the Vedic scriptures, and include the many avatars of Vishnu who come into this world to teach, inspire, protect, and show love to the living beings.

'Krishna journeys through these countless worlds of matter to reveal his personal beauty and love. In all these worlds He shows himself and his deeds. Just as the sun illuminates every far-flung corner of this globe—somewhere rising, somewhere standing at noon, and somewhere setting—so Krishna shows himself and his deeds throughout these worlds. The soul has partial sight of Krishna in this world, just as one might glimpse the moon through the branches of a tree—the moon appears caught among the branches but is far beyond them.

'Krishna's spiritual potency is spread as an endless luminous sky filled with effulgent planets more numerous than the atoms of this universe. These eternal planets cluster like lotus petals about the whorl of Krishna's personal home, Goloka Vrindavan.'

As he spoke, his ecstasy overflowed. He sang two verses from the *Bhagavatam* in praise of Krishna's beauty:

'Krishna appears in this world like a rain cloud in the sky: his pearl necklace is like a row of white ducks, his peacock feather like a rainbow, his yellow garments flash like lightning. His sweet pastimes shower upon us as rains fall upon the parched fields.

'Unable to see enough of Krishna's beauty, the gopis in the forest criticised the creator—"How inconsiderate is Brahma. He gave us only two eyes, when we wish to see Krishna with thousands of eyes; and even these two eyes keep blinking, so preventing us from seeing Krishna's sweetness at every second."

'Krishna's potencies are like the limitless ocean. My words can touch only a drop of them.'

So concluded his first teaching, the soul and its relationship with Krishna. He continued.

2

'YOU HAVE HEARD about the soul's relationship with Krishna. Now hear how to reawaken that relationship.

'Most souls are forever free in the realm of spirit: only some choose to turn away from Krishna, and so are bound by matter. In pursuit of their desires they enter material bodies and wander in the cycle of rebirth, in which they pass countless lifetimes suffering the pangs of mortal existence. If they are fortunate they meet a true teacher who can set them on the path of freedom from the bonds of birth and death. This freedom is found through following the way of service and devotion, giving oneself to Krishna in love.

'The six ways of surrender to Krishna are:

1. *Accept what is favourable for Krishna's service*
2. *Avoid what is unfavourable for his service*
3. *Have full faith in his protection*
4. *Feel confident he will always maintain you*
5. *Depend on his will even when you don't understand it*
6. *Always be humble before the Lord*

'Service to Krishna begins with seeking the shelter of a Krishna conscious person who is attached to the loving service of the Lord. Here are some of the qualities of such a person:

+ Kind to everyone
+ Does not pick a quarrel with anyone
+ Takes the essence of life, spiritual life
+ Equal to all
+ No one can find fault in the devotee
+ The mind is always fresh and clean
+ Free from material desires
+ A benefactor to all
+ Humble and fixed in purpose
+ Victorious over lust and anger
+ Does not over-eat
+ Respectful to all but does not require respect
+ Grave
+ Silent
+ Expert
+ Poetic
+ Peaceful
+ A merciful friend to all
+ Surrendered to Krishna

'One moment in the company of such a pure lover of Krishna is enough to bring you success.

'Guided by your teacher, practice devotional service following these five principles:

1. Associate with devotees
2. Chant the holy names of God
3. Hear or read the holy Srimad Bhagavatam
4. Live in Vrindavan or near a temple of Krishna
5. Worship the deity of Krishna

'Pure love for Krishna lives in the heart of every being. When your heart is cleansed by service, love awakens naturally. In this awakened state you can offer your love to Krishna in everything you do: in hearing, chanting, remembering, worshipping, praying, serving, obeying, in friendship, or in surrendering your whole life to him. Most important among these nine are the first three: hearing, chanting and remembering.

'When love awakens, a person is no longer bound by any rule, and service becomes spontaneous. At this point the devotee is attracted to remember a particular companion of Krishna in Vrindavan, and to follow in the footsteps of that divine person, meditating with deep absorption upon that blessed one's service to Krishna.'

With these words he completed his second teaching, how to revive that eternal relationship. He went on.

3

'I HAVE SPOKEN of the path for reviving the soul's eternal relationship with Krishna. Now I will tell you of life's ultimate goal: love of Godhead.

'With faith seek the company of pure souls. So one is initiated into the practice of devotional service. Unwanted habits diminish, and faith becomes firmly established in one's heart. So comes deep taste and attachment to the spiritual life. In time spiritual emotions intensify and pure love awakens. When affection for Krishna deepens to love, it shines like a ray of sunlight and softens the heart with spiritual emotions. A devotee in love with Krishna shows forgiveness, care for use of time, detachment, freedom from pride, hope, eagerness, taste for Krishna's name, attachment to hearing about Krishna, and affection for the holy places of Krishna.

'In this stage a pure lover of Krishna loudly chants Krishna's name, and laughs or cries, not caring what others think, being absorbed in loving Krishna in one of the five primary relationships. Waves of ecstasy mix together, stimulated by Krishna's beauty and by Krishna's loving associates.

'Among all the Lord's loving companions Radha is the heroine. She smiles brightly, she is humble, and she submits to the love of her friends. Yet she has Krishna under her control and is the most dear to Krishna. She is full of mercy.

'All these spiritual emotions and loving affairs can only be understood by pure lovers of Krishna.'

So ended his third teaching, the ultimate goal of life.

FOR TWO MONTHS Mahaprabhu taught Sanatan, blessing him with divine understanding. Sanatan and his brother Rupa went on to write books inspired by all they had learned from Sri Chaitanya Mahaprabhu. Whoever in years to come would hear and study these teachings would learn the complete path of *bhaktiyoga*, devotional service to Krishna, the essence of Sri Chaitanya's teaching.

Mahaprabhu gave a dual mission to Sanatan: to educate people through writing books, and to uncover the holy places of Krishna's pastimes in Vrindavan. In giving Sanatan these tasks he emphasised that the way to real freedom in this world is to see everything and everyone in relation to Krishna.

AS LONG AS MAHAPRABHU STAYED in Varanasi the people of the town talked about him. They mostly favoured the *Advaita* philosophy of non-dualism, as taught by the great teacher Shankara who had lived seven hundred years earlier. His commentary on Vedanta held that all beings are one with God, and that individual personality and form, including the personality and form of Krishna, are part of the illusion called *maya*, 'that which is not.' Followers of this philosophy were hence called *mayavadis*. The *mayavadi* sannyasis of Varanasi were devoted to silent meditation and philosophical study. They were not given to personal devotion, for they saw Krishna as part of the illusion. Their life of yoga was based around penance and austerity, renouncing all kinds of enjoyment. They saw singing the glories of God in public, as Mahaprabhu and his followers did, as an indulgence for beginners. They openly said Chaitanya was a sentimentalist. He didn't complain, he simply avoided them and waited for the right time, when he would share his love with them and teach them the eternal truth of devotion. He had become a sannyasi to meet such people on equal terms and speak to them about Krishna. Now he waited patiently.

Meanwhile his small community of devotees in Varanasi daily heard criticisms of their beloved master. They felt unhappy and begged him to do something. If his critics would meet him personally and hear from him, they believed, their hearts would change. They would not have to wait long. A well-to-do brahmin decided to invite all the sannyasis of Varanasi to his home for lunch. He received acceptances from them all, including their leader Prakasananda Sarasvati.

He then came personally to invite Sri Chaitanya.

On the appointed day a large crowd of monks gathered at the brahmin's house. Led by Prakasananda they sat in a big circle, waiting in anticipation to meet the young sannyasi Sri Krishna Chaitanya, whom they had heard so much about. When he entered all eyes turned upon him. Although he was younger than them all, his commanding presence filled the room. He was broad-shouldered and taller than anyone they had seen; when he bowed to offer them his respects, the sannyasis heard his deep voice resonate with authority.

In expectant silence they watched this effulgent golden personality, whose beautiful face shone like the moon, sit on the bare floor at the entrance, by the place for washing feet. As one they rose with dismay and wonder. He should not sit there by the door—he should have a seat of honour in their midst. Prakasananda hurried over and took his hand.

'Your holiness, please do not sit there.'

'I belong to a lower order of sannyasis. I do not deserve to sit with you.'

'No, please come and take the place of honour,' insisted Prakasananda, leading him into the midst of their assembly.

Once Mahaprabhu was seated, Prakasananda questioned him in front of everyone.

'Krishna Chaitanya, you are a sannyasi like us, and you belong to our lineage of Shankara, yet why are you avoiding us? I have another question. A sannyasi is supposed to spend his time in meditation and study of Vedanta, so why do you sing and dance in public, surrounding yourself with common people and religious sentimentalists? Please explain yourself.'

Mahaprabhu paused and smiled at the assembled sannyasis. Then he spoke with a clear and calm voice.

LIFE'S ULTIMATE PERFECTION

'MY TEACHER TOLD ME I am not qualified to study Vedanta. Instead he advised me to chant the names of Krishna. He said chanting Krishna's names is sufficient to release me from the cycle of birth and death and bring me to Lord Krishna's lotus feet. He taught me a verse from the scriptures:

"Chant the holy name, chant the holy name, chant the holy name—in this age of Kali there is no other way, no other way, no other way to achieve success."

'Since hearing these words I have not stopped chanting. At first I thought I was losing my mind. I found myself helplessly singing, dancing, laughing and crying. So I asked my teacher what was happening. He told me I was experiencing spiritual ecstasy, the sign of love of God, which is the true result of chanting Krishna's name. In comparison with the ocean of bliss found in Krishna's name, the joy of your impersonal realisation is a shallow pond. All this my teacher told me. He urged me to go on chanting and dancing in the company of devotees, without caring what others thought, to teach this practice of sankirtan and so save all the people.'

Mahaprabhu's audience felt a great attraction to him and were pleased by his words. But they were deeply committed to Vedanta philosophy—it was the foundation for their whole way of life.

'We like what you say,' said Prakasananda, 'and we are happy for you because you have achieved love for God. But why do you avoid studying the Vedanta?'

'The verses of the *Vedanta Sutra* were spoken by Lord Narayana himself, and they are without fault,' answered Mahaprabhu. 'It is not the verses that I avoid, but the interpretations placed upon them by Shankara. I mean no disrespect to Shankara, for he is an incarnation of Shiva, but I disagree profoundly with his teaching. The Supreme Lord's form is eternal and spiritual, whereas Shankara said it is temporary and made of illusion.

'We are eternal sparks of the Supreme Lord, and are forever individuals. The individual soul can never be equal to the original Supreme Soul. We are energy, while God is the source of energy—we are *shakti* and God is *shaktiman*. We are eternal servants, while God is the eternal Lord. On this truth, taught in the Vedanta, Shankara has misled people. Therefore I say it is better to hear the original verses of the Vedanta, which all point to Sri Krishna, than to hear Shankara's indirect interpretations. Whoever hears those interpretations is lost.'

Although Mahaprabhu's words contradicted the Mayavadi doctrines, he was voicing doubts many of them stored in their minds. They wanted to hear more.

'What your holiness says is true,' Prakasananda said. 'We also are not satisfied with the indirect explanations of our texts. Now please tell us the direct meaning of the *Vedanta Sutra*.'

Mahaprabhu replied.

'The Great Spirit described in the Vedanta is the Supreme Personality of Godhead, who possesses all qualities and is the source of all truth. By making God impersonal, Shankara has denied God's full spiritual nature. The only way to reach the Supreme Person is to hear about the qualities of that Supreme Being with devotion under the guidance of a spiritual teacher. Then your natural love for God will manifest, free from material attachment. Such love is the highest goal, for it attracts Krishna and brings the sweet taste of devotional service. Your relationship with God, how to develop that relationship, and the perfection of love for God—these three subjects are described in every verse of the *Vedanta Sutra*.'

'The author of the *Vedanta Sutra* is Vyasadeva. His teacher was Narada Muni, who heard from Brahma, the first created being in the universe, who was taught by Vishnu himself. Vyasadeva summarised the essential truths of the four Vedas and the Upanishads in the verses of the Vedanta Sutras, then he explained their meaning in *Srimad Bhagavatam*, the perfect commentary on the Vedanta and the Upanishads. In the *Bhagavatam* he revealed three great truths: the essence of all relationships is Krishna; the essential activity is *bhakti*, devotional service to Krishna; and ultimate perfection is *prema*, love for Krishna.'

Mahaprabhu finished speaking. His words left a profound affect, changing forever the hearts of all present. From that day they began to chant Krishna's names, and no more criticisms of Mahaprabhu were heard in Varanasi.

PEOPLE ALL OVER TOWN talked about Mahaprabhu and discussed his teachings. Many came to debate with him personally. Each one of them was welcomed with respect. Mahaprabhu would convince them with reason and logic to develop a personal understanding of God, and to take up the practice of *bhaktiyoga*. Soon, the Mayavadi sannyasis gathered at their ashram to discuss all they had heard. One of their elders voiced his feelings.

'Sri Krishna Chaitanya is right. To renounce the world without taking up devotional service to Krishna is like beating an empty husk: your labour will be fruitless. Therefore, I say, we should follow his teaching and worship Krishna's divine form. For Krishna is himself the ultimate Brahman and the cause of everything.' Prakasananda heard these words and approved.

'The conclusion of the Vedanta is that the Ultimate Truth is personal,' asserted Prakasananda. 'Shankaracarya denied this, and therefore his interpretations are misleading. We prefer to accept the words of Sri Krishna Chaitanya, who speaks the truth.' After saying this, he himself led the sannyasis out onto the street while chanting Krishna's names.

There they found Mahaprabhu chanting and dancing in great ecstasy with Chandrasekhar, Tapana Misra and many others. When Mahaprabhu saw Prakasananda and his followers approaching, he stopped his chanting and bowed to the senior monk. But Prakasananda bowed lower, touching his forehead to the ground before him.

'Forgive me Lord,' he begged. 'Before our meeting I said many ungenerous things about you. Now by touching your feet I hope to be freed from my offences, for you are the Supreme Lord Krishna himself.'

Mahaprabhu protested, saying he was simply a servant of Krishna. He advised Prakasananda to study *Srimad Bhagavatam* and always to chant the names of Krishna. In this way he would achieve not just liberation, but the ultimate perfection of *prema*, pure love for God.

For the remainder of Mahaprabhu's stay in Varanasi, Prakasananda and the other sannyasis came regularly to see him and chant with him in public. One day Mahaprabhu visited the temple of Visvesvara, dedicated to Shiva, in the heart of the town. A huge crowd gathered and followed him down to the riverside. There he raised his hands to the sky and everyone began to sing. The air was filled with the sound of Krishna's names. So it was that the people of Varanasi joined one another in singing the holy names, and the town became like a second Navadvipa.

IT WAS NEARLY TIME for Mahaprabhu to return to Jagannath Puri. He had been away for almost six months and the hot season was approaching. His devotees in Varanasi wanted to come with him, but he asked them to stay behind. Later they could visit him, he said, but he wanted to return as he had come, travelling alone through the forest of Jarikhanda.

Before leaving he spoke one last time with Sanatan. When they first met in Ramakeli he had accepted him as his disciple, and given him the name Sanatan. Now he made him Sanatan Goswami, recognising him as one who has mastered his body and mind, and is thus qualified to lead others. Mahaprabhu repeated his earlier wish that Sanatan should live in Vrindavan to uncover the holy places and write books. Mahaprabhu added to this a further request. In the future, he said, devotees from all over India would come to Vrindavan, either to visit or to stay. Many of them would be poor and destitute, having left everything to seek Krishna. He asked Sanatan to organise shelter and spiritual support for all these devotees.

Following this direction Sanatan Goswami dedicated the remainder of his life to caring for devotees in Vrindavan. His skill and experience in public affairs, coupled with his deep knowledge in the scriptures, made him the ideal person to lead the Vaishnava community there. Above all these qualities were his natural compassion, deep humility and devotion.

Sanatan gave up all comforts to live in Vrindavan as a mendicant. He wandered among the twelve forests, shunning permanent shelter, preferring to sleep beneath trees or among bushes. As he moved around he collected the sacred history of the area, reviving the holy places of Krishna's life, comforting and guiding, and writing profound literatures about Krishna consciousness. Wherever he went he always remembered Krishna.

MAHAPRABHU PASSED THROUGH the forests of Jarikhanda and reached the outskirts of Jagannath Puri. There he halted while word of his arrival was sent to his devoted followers. In great excitement they came out to greet him with tears, embraces and much laughter and joy. They brought him to the temple where with great ecstasy he saw Jagannath, the priests coming out with garlands and offerings from the deities. Finally Mahaprabhu was taken to his rooms at Kasi Misra's house. There a feast was shared in his honour by Sarvabhauma Bhattacarya and Svarupa Damodara, while his devotees gathered, their joy overflowing.

Sri Chaitanya was thirty years old. His outward travels were over. Now he would stay in Puri in the company of his friends. For the remainder of his life his journey led him inwards, to the everlasting realm of Radha and Krishna.

12

CARE AMONG FRIENDS

RUPA HELD ONTO THE SACRED WORDS he had received from his lord and master. With sorrow in his heart, he and his brother Anupama left the confluence at Prayag and set off for Vrindavan. As they walked Rupa contemplated what was now his life's mission: to write books and poems exploring the eternal realm of pure love for Krishna. Upon reaching Vrindavan, the brothers toured the twelve forests following in the footsteps of Sri Chaitanya, all the while Rupa seeking inspiration for his writing and wondering how he would begin. He felt inspired to compose a drama about the love between Krishna and his companions in Vrindavan.

His drama would depict the love of Radha and Krishna in the forest of Vrindavan alongside the love of Queen Satyabhama and Krishna in the city of Dvaraka. He wanted to reveal Krishna's different sides: as cowherd boy in the forest and royal prince in Dvaraka; to contrast the intimate love of Vrindavan with the reverential love of the royal city.

He composed some verses, but without the company of his elder brother he was uncertain how to proceed. He longed to be with Mahaprabhu again to seek further guidance and encouragement.

Rupa and Anupama heard Mahaprabhu was in Varanasi and decided to return there, hoping to see him before he left. But by the time they arrived their master had already departed for Puri. They also found that Sanatan had recently been in Varanasi and was now making his way to Vrindavan by a different route—they had crossed paths without either of them knowing. Missing his older brother, Rupa decided to follow Mahaprabhu all the way to Puri. After staying a few days in Varanasi as guests of Mahaprabhu's followers, Rupa and Anupama continued on their way, stopping in Bengal to visit their family members in Ramakeli. While they were in Bengal fate intervened. Anupama, faithful friend and helper to his older brothers, and recipient of Mahaprabhu's mercy, fell ill and passed away by the banks of the Ganges.

Bereft of his brother's company, Rupa pressed on alone for Jagannath Puri, his thoughts dwelling ever more on his service to his master. He was seeking inspiration on how best to structure his drama, when one night he was visited by a powerful dream in which a beautiful goddess appeared and blessed him.

'Write a drama just about me,' she said, 'and I promise you it will be wonderful.'

On waking, Rupa believed he had been blessed directly by Satyabhama. Her wishes were clear: whereas he had planned to write a single drama, she wanted him to write two separate works, one about Krishna as cowherd boy in Vrindavan, and the other about Krishna the royal prince in Dvaraka. Satyabhama, her spirited personality revealed in the pages of the *Bhagavatam*, would make an absorbing focus for his drama set in Dvaraka, and would complement the story of Radha's love for Krishna in the groves of Vrindavan. Though Rupa saw this, he was unsure how to proceed—he needed to hear from his master.

When he reached Puri he found the town full of Mahaprabhu's followers from Bengal, there to celebrate Rathayatra as they did every year. Rupa felt self-conscious. Puri was a seat of Hindu orthodoxy, and in this setting he was made aware of his former Muslim associations. Although he was born a high-caste Hindu, he had lived and worked among Muslims as if he were one of them. The first time he visited Chaitanya in Ramakeli he had been in the Nawab's service. Then he had met Chaitanya's companion Haridas Thakur and learned of his Muslim background.

Now in Puri, Rupa sought out Haridas's company. He found him in his modest shelter near the seashore. Here the elderly Haridas spent his whole time absorbed in his daily recitation of Krishna's names three hundred thousand times according to his vow. He gladly welcomed Rupa into his small shelter and gave this cultured young Vaishnava a place to stay, promising he would soon meet his dear master.

Rupa would not have long to wait, for it was Mahaprabhu's custom each day to visit Haridas. His routine was to witness Jagannath's lunchtime offering at the temple, then bathe in the sea and recite his noon mantras. On his way down to the beach he would bring Haridas prasadam from the temple, and speak with him. So it was, at noon on the very day of Rupa's arrival, that Mahaprabhu appeared at Haridas's cottage.

'Rupa has come to see you,' said Haridas, and Rupa prostrated himself in the sand.

Mahaprabhu was pleased to see his young disciple again, and spoke with him for a while. He asked after Rupa's brothers and heard of the untimely death of Anupama, and how Rupa and Sanatan had missed each other on the road.

The following day Mahaprabhu introduced Rupa to the devotees, and asked Advaita Acarya and Nityananda, as the two leading Bengali Vaishnavas, to give him their blessings to write about *bhaktirasa*, the emotions of divine love.

Rupa settled in and absorbed himself in writing his poetry. One day, while Chaitanya was with Haridas, he said something special to Rupa.

'Krishna never leaves Vrindavan. When he is away from Vrindavan he becomes Vasudeva Krishna, who is different from the original Krishna.'

Rupa thought deeply about his master's words. They echoed what he had heard in his dream of Satyabhama—that in his writings he must keep Krishna in Vrindavan apart from Krishna in Dvaraka, putting a distance between the intimate atmosphere of Vrindavan and the more formal atmosphere of Dvaraka. He resolved to divide his drama into two distinct works.

Rupa longed to receive further guidance from Mahaprabhu. He wanted to know if his compositions would be pleasing to him. His opportunity came in an unexpected way.

At the time of Rathayatra, Rupa witnessed Chaitanya's dance of ecstasy in front of Jagannath. He heard Mahaprabhu sing the words of Radha—words that until now only Svarupa Damodara had comprehended. When Rupa heard Chaitanya sing this verse he understood instinctively the whole context of his master's words—why he sang as Radha and what memories the words evoked.

Hurrying to his cottage absorbed in these thoughts, Rupa composed a verse to express Radha's conflicting feelings of love for Krishna. He wrote in the voice of Radha.

'Hear me dear friend. I have met my lover of old here on the field of Kurukshetra. I am the same Radha and he is the same Krishna. We are meeting in happiness as before. But still I long to be with him beneath the trees in the forest of Vrindavan, beside the bank of the Yamuna. There I can hear him play that fifth note on his sweet flute.'

He inscribed this verse on a palm leaf and hid it within the thatched roof of his cottage, before leaving to bathe in the sea. While he was gone Mahaprabhu arrived and saw the palm leaf. Taking it down he read it and was astonished by what Rupa had written, so he waited for his return.

'Dear Rupa, how could you know what was in my heart?'

Rupa could only bow in silent humility.

'You have blessed him with your special mercy,' said Svarupa. 'For your inner thoughts are a secret none can guess.'

'Rupa came to me in Prayag,' replied Mahaprabhu.

'There I empowered him to reveal many truths about Krishna. Now, while he is with us here in Puri, I want you to teach him all you know about *bhaktirasa*.'

Svarupa gladly accepted this request. He began to spend time with Rupa, speaking about the loving affairs of Radha and Krishna. Together they brought them alive and entered ever deeper into the unending transcendental realm of pure love. So Rupa stayed in Puri for many months. After the devotees from Bengal had all returned to their homes, he was still there receiving inspiration and guidance for writing his two dramas.

One day Mahaprabhu came to see Rupa and Haridas. He saw some palm leaves inscribed in Rupa's fair hand, and held them up.

'Rupa Goswami's handwriting is like a row of pearls,' he declared, and began reading. As he read from the leaves one particular verse caught his attention. It was in praise of the holy name of Krishna, and was full of musical sounds, rhythm and alliteration. With great pleasure he sang aloud the Sanskrit lines.

'tunde tandavini ratim vitanute tundavali labdhaye
karna kroda kadambini ghatayate karnarbudebhyah sriham
cetah prangana sangini vijayate sarvendriyanam kritim
no jane janita kiyadbhir amritaih krishneti varna dvayi'

'I do not know how much nectar these two syllables
krish-na *have produced. When the name of Krishna is*
chanted, it dances within the mouth and we desire
many, many mouths. The name enters the ears and we
desire many millions of ears. When the name dances in
the courtyard of the heart, it conquers the activities of
the mind, and all the senses become inert.'

When Haridas heard this verse he cried for joy. His sole occupation was to chant Krishna's names day and night, and he had never heard such a poetic description of the experience of chanting. After discovering this verse, Mahaprabhu wanted his companions to hear the beauty of Rupa's poetry. The following day he brought Svarupa, Sarvabhauma and Ramananda to the cottage.

He sat them down and asked Rupa to chant the verse that had so impressed him after Rathayatra. Rupa was too modest to speak, so Svarupa sang it for him. When the others heard the verse describing Radha's longing to be with Krishna in Vrindavan they understood, as Svarupa had before them, that such deep insights into the mind of Mahaprabhu were possible only for one who had received his special blessing. They persuaded Rupa to chant his verse in glorification of Krishna's name. Upon hearing it, everyone was full of praise.

Ramananda, who was thought by all to be the expert on *rasa*, wanted to question Rupa. What else was he writing, and would he share more of his poetry? Rupa was hesitant, but he was persuaded to share some of his poetic jewels. The more he revealed, the more his audience became stunned. Their respect grew for this gentle young Vaishnava whose words spoke so profoundly of the deep emotions of the soul in a way that touched their hearts. For a long time the company sat together, sharing different feelings of transcendental love. They heard verses taken from the opening scenes of Rupa's two dramas, first describing Vrindavan, then Krishna, then Radharani and her innermost thoughts. Rupa was uplifted by the loving appreciation he was given, yet humbled by such attention from these exalted souls.

'In your presence I feel overwhelmed, like a glow-worm in the presence of the sun,' he said. Still Ramananda urged him on. Rupa made the Sanskrit language sing as he evoked the subtleties of spiritual emotions, just as Mahaprabhu had known he would. The devotees gave Rupa their affectionate blessings, and in response he could only praise his teacher, Sri Krishna Chaitanya.

Rupa stayed with Haridas a few days more, then it was time for him to leave. He had been in Puri for ten months, during which time he was accepted into his master's inner circle of associates and enriched with countless blessings.

'Now go to Vrindavan and stay there,' Mahaprabhu bade him. 'Write wonderful books and help Sanatan uncover Krishna's holy places. Together the two of you will teach everyone about devotional service to Krishna. One day I will come and visit you there. Until then, serve me in that holy place.' And he added, 'Tell Sanatan he also should come here to visit me.'

He embraced Rupa, who fell to the ground weeping, with his head placed at his master's feet. With fond farewells ringing in his ears he left, travelling first to Bengal then on to Vrindavan.

In the years that followed, having heard the secrets of devotional service from Sri Chaitanya Mahaprabhu, and blessed by him and his devotees to realise these truths in his heart, Rupa Goswami wrote many books. His two dramas about Krishna in Vrindavan and Dvaraka, named *Vidagdha-Madhava* and *Lalita-Madhava*, were completed. His greatest work was entitled *Bhakti Rasamrita Sindhu*, The Ocean of the Nectar of Devotion. It is the definitive treatise on the complete art of *bhaktirasa*. Its opening words are:

'Insignificant though I am, I pray to the lotus feet of Sri Chaitanya, the Supreme Lord in my heart. He inspired me to write this book.'

EVEN AS RUPA MADE HIS WAY back to Bengal and Vrindavan, his brother Sanatan was traversing the jungles and stony terrain of central India. Like Rupa, he had stayed for some time in Vrindavan before setting off to visit Sri Chaitanya in Jagannath Puri. He followed the same cross-country route taken by Mahaprabhu earlier that year because he wanted to avoid being seen in Bengal. By the time he reached Jagannath Puri he was weak from fasting and had developed a skin infection after being forced to drink contaminated water while alone in the forest. He felt acutely uncomfortable as he approached Puri. In addition to the infectious sores on his skin, he believed himself an outcast among Hindus because of his former involvement with their Muslim rulers.

'What is the use of this wretched body?' he thought despairingly. 'No one wants me here, and I will not even be able to see my Lord Chaitanya, because he lives among the high-caste priests close to the temple.' Filled with these gloomy thoughts he resolved to put an end to his life by throwing himself beneath the wheels of Jagannath's chariot in the presence of his divine master.

As Rupa had done before him, Sanatan went in search of Haridas Thakur, as the one he knew and trusted to understand his feelings. Haridas welcomed him to his cottage and embraced him as a dear friend. When Mahaprabhu came to visit he was surprised to find Sanatan there. He opened his arms to embrace his beloved devotee, but Sanatan shrank away.

'Don't touch me Lord, I beg you. I am an outcast and my body is covered with weeping sores. Just let me lie in the dust at your feet.'

Despite these words Mahaprabhu held Sanatan tight, then introduced him to his companions.

Sanatan stayed with Haridas and time passed. Together they chanted Krishna's names and from a distance looked upon the pinnacle of Jagannath's temple. This was the nearest either of them permitted themselves to go because they knew the caste brahmins of Jagannath Puri forbade temple access to non-Hindus. But each day Mahaprabhu came to see them. He brought them prasadam from the temple and stayed to talk about Krishna.

One day, to Sanatan's surprise, Mahaprabhu brought up the topic of suicide.

'It is true that a devotee who loves Krishna finds it hard to be apart from Him in this world, and so sometimes desires death. But to deliberately take your own life will never bring you closer to Krishna. The only way to reach Krishna is through loving service. Don't think your body is unfit for serving Krishna. No one is disqualified from the Lord's service, not even the most insignificant person in the eyes of this world. By serving Krishna you become exalted, whereas the greatest people of this world, if they do not serve Krishna, are of no consequence. *There are many ways to serve Krishna. Best is to chant his name in all humility, for that will bring you the gift of pure love.* Give up your morbid thoughts and chant Krishna's names. Then you will achieve his shelter.'

Sanatan heard these words and fell at his master's feet.

'You knew all that was in my mind, Lord. I am indeed the lowest—what use can I be to you?'

'Your body belongs to me. Through you I have important work to do. You will teach many things: how to be a devotee; how to love Krishna; the character and behaviour of Vaishnavas. And you will establish pilgrimage places in my sacred homeland of Mathura and Vrindavan.'

Sanatan was astonished to hear all this. In wonder he prayed.

'Lord, make me your instrument. Please make me dance, like a puppet who dances without knowing what he is doing.'

Placing Sanatan under the watchful care of Haridas, Mahaprabhu embraced them both and left. Watching him leave, Haridas rejoiced for Sanatan.

'Your good fortune cannot be measured, for all these things will certainly come to pass. You will do wonderful service for the Lord. As for me, I am of no use.'

'But Haridas, no one chants Krishna's name with more faith and devotion than you. Each day you chant three hundred thousand holy names. Through you the Lord is teaching everyone. Some live good lives but do not teach, others teach but do not live well. You, however, do both and you are ideal in every way.'

So the two passed their time encouraging one another in mutual love.

The summer heat arrived and sands along the seashore baked under the blazing sun. One day Mahaprabhu sent for Sanatan to join him for lunch in a favourite seaside garden. Not wanting to pass in front of the temple gate, Sanatan walked along the beach. He was so intent on seeing his beloved master that he disregarded any pain from the hot sand. By the time he reached the garden his feet were blistered and burned. Mahaprabhu was dismayed, but he understood Sanatan's motive was to avoid passing the temple entrance, so as not to disturb the servants of Jagannath.

'Sanatan, only you have the humility to behave like this, showing respect even when it gives your body pain. Such good behaviour is the ornament of a devotee.' Mahaprabhu reached out and embraced him, despite Sanatan's reluctance to allow his master to touch his diseased body. On this and other occasions Sanatan felt blessed by the Lord's affections, but he was unhappy. He confided in Haridas that he could not stay in Puri because he was causing offences by letting his master embrace him. News of Sanatan's misgivings reached Mahaprabhu's ears and he decided he must console him.

'My dear Sanatan, I feel deep regard and affection for you—please do not leave yet. You are deeply learned in the scriptures, with the power to teach even me. I love you just like my own child. Your weeping sores offend me no more than a baby's mess offends its mother. Like a mother, I find you faultless. To me your body is all spiritual. Now let me bless you.' So saying, he embraced Sanatan yet again. At that moment, as his Lord embraced him, Sanatan's sores vanished and his skin glowed golden. From that day he was cured.

Summer passed and Sanatan lamented no more. Again it was time for Rathayatra, when he met the devotees from Bengal and they befriended him as they had Rupa. After their departure he remained with Mahaprabhu until the day came for him to return to Vrindavan. His parting with Sri Chaitanya held joy mixed with sadness, for they would not meet again in this life.

Sanatan retraced his footsteps through Jarikhanda Forest. He stopped at all the places where Mahaprabhu had halted and heard about him from the local inhabitants. A year after his original departure he arrived back in Vrindavan. There he was joined by his brother Rupa who had settled their family affairs in Bengal and returned to Vrindavan for good.

The two brothers worked together in Vrindavan for the rest of days, serving Mahaprabhu's orders. They gathered scriptures and unearthed lost holy places associated with the life of Krishna. They established beautiful temples, particularly the temple dedicated to Madana Mohan founded by Sanatan, and the temple dedicated to Govinda founded by Rupa. For themselves they needed no comforts. They lived with utmost simplicity, depending on the charity of householders as they moved from one forest grove to another without permanent shelter. They preferred to sleep beneath the stars, sheltered by the sacred trees of Vrindavan, and so spent their time serving Krishna's devotees, writing books and chanting Krishna's names.

Sanatan Goswami's most important book was the *Brihad Bhagavatamrita*, which taught everything as Mahaprabhu had asked him. In it, through story and through wisdom from the *Bhagavatam*, he entered the eternal spiritual reality, teaching who is a devotee, how to perform devotional service, and revealing truths about Krishna. He also wrote *Sri Krishna Lila Stava*, a poetic meditation on Krishna's life in Vrindavan, and *Hari Bhakti Vilasa*, in which he taught how to live in this world as a devotee of Krishna. These books became the foundation for the Krishna consciousness movement in years to come.

THROUGH THE LIFE OF RAGHUNATH, Chaitanya taught one of the different ways of spiritual life. Most of his followers were householders who lived with their families and offered whatever they could in devotion to Krishna. For them his instruction was to practice Krishna consciousness at home.

'Stay at home and always chant Krishna's holy names,' he had told the brahmin in Kurmakshetra. 'And tell whomever you meet about Krishna's teachings.'

Others among his followers chose to renounce home and family, and from them he expected serious commitment. He taught this through his own life as well as through the lives of the sannyasis who were close to him. Among them one who gave up all forms of comfort was Raghunath Das. His story offers a glimpse into the depth of unworldly detachment found in some of Chaitanya's surrendered followers. Raghunath's example is not for everyone, but his life shows just how far a person may be inspired to go to enter the most rarefied realms of pure love for Krishna.

He grew up in an extremely wealthy Vaishnava family who lived near Navadvipa, and were related to Chaitanya's family. As a young boy Raghunath met Haridas Thakur and was inspired by his example toward a life of renunciation and devotion to Krishna. When he was nineteen he went to see Sri Chaitanya at Advaita's house when the Master was returning from his first attempt to reach Vrindavan. On that occasion Raghunath was set on renouncing the world to be with his master in Puri. Sri Chaitanya told him to be patient and to wait until the right time, when Krishna would surely release him from his family obligations.

During the next two years, while Chaitanya successfully made his pilgrimage to Vrindavan, the young Raghunath stayed patiently in his family home. He executed his father's bidding, which meant handling large amounts of money, for his father Govardhana was a wealthy landowner. But Raghunath became increasingly unhappy. His father tried all ways to encourage him to settle down, giving him gold, luxuries and servants, and arranging his marriage to a beautiful girl. But, like Prince Siddhartha long before him, he thought only of how he could be free from all material ties. His only desire was to be with his worshipful Lord.

Three years passed, and news reached Raghunath that Sri Chaitanya had finished his travels and returned to Puri. Raghunath's restlessness increased; he could no longer tolerate being trapped at home. He made a bid for freedom, slipping away under cover of darkness, but his father sent out a search party and had him brought back.

Several times he tried to escape, until his father placed him under constant guard.

One day Raghunath heard that Nityananda was staying with a party of devotees in the nearby village of Panihati. He thought if he went and petitioned him he might receive some help. So he got permission to visit there with a group of his father's servants. He found Nityananda by the Ganges sitting beneath a great tree, glowing like the sun amid a crowd of followers. Hoping to remain anonymous, Raghunath hid at the back, where he fell to the ground in reverence. But he was recognised.

'Look! Here is Raghunath, come to see you,' called one of the devotees, and Nityananda knew him at once.

'Raghunath, why are you hiding? Come here and I will punish you!' Amid laughter Raghunath was pulled to the front, where Nityananda placed his feet on Raghunath's head.

'I want you to feed all these devotees with yoghurt and chipped rice,' he commanded.

Chipped rice was the staple food in poor Bengali villages, but when he heard this command Raghunath enthusiastically set about making it the main ingredient for a wonderful feast. He sent his servants into the village to buy rice, yoghurt, milk, sugar, bananas and sweets. They gathered hundreds of clay pots and organised a great festival to feed whoever came. As word spread people flooded in from the surrounding villages and Raghunath bought whatever was available from the nearby markets. Soon there were so many to feed that some of them even had to stand in the river.

At the height of the celebrations, Nityananda in a mood of ecstasy meditated upon Chaitanya, calling him to come and witness the glorious scene. In a spiritual form Sri Chaitanya manifested in response. Nityananda walked with him through the crowd of seated devotees, talking and laughing with his unseen companion and offering him food as they went. There were some fortunate souls who were blessed also to see Chaitanya. They saw their two Lords seated side by side, eating together just like Krishna and Balarama surrounded by cowherd boys on the bank of the Yamuna River. This wonderful scene was impressed deeply on the minds of all present, and forever afterwards the day was remembered by Vaishnavas as the Panihati chipped rice festival.

When they had finished eating, the devotees sang and danced in ecstasy, chanting Krishna's names. In the centre of the gathering Nityananda danced in his unique way that no one could imitate, with a sweetness surpassing description.

Raghunath, filled with happiness to have been given this opportunity to serve Nityananda, stayed all that day and night with the devotees, and in the morning came before Nityananda to reveal his mind.

'I long to be with my Lord Chaitanya. This is all I can think of. But it seems impossible. I feel like a dwarf who wants to catch the moon. Whenever I try to get away from my family they bring me back. If you bless me, though I am not worthy, I will be able to achieve the shelter of Sri Chaitanya.'

'Just observe Raghunath,' said Nityananda to his companions. 'He lives like the king of heaven with every imaginable comfort, yet he thinks only of leaving. All of you give him your blessings so he can get the mercy of Mahaprabhu.' Then he turned to Raghunath. 'Sri Chaitanya came here just to give you his mercy. He awaits you in Puri, where I foresee that you will become one of his dearest servants. Go home now, and very soon you will be freed to join him.'

With these words of encouragement Raghunath returned home. From that day he gave up his bed and slept on the veranda beside the family shrine, always thinking of how to escape the watchful eyes of his guards. One night his chance arrived when he was asked to help at the nearby temple. He went there in the evening and suddenly found himself without a guard. Though unprepared, with nothing but the clothes he wore, he sped into the darkness.

Avoiding roads and villages he moved swiftly through the jungle. By nightfall the following day he was thirty miles away. He met a cowherd who let him stay the night in his cowshed and fed him some milk. He pressed on, hardly eating or resting, and in only twelve days covered the distance to Jagannath Puri. By the time he reached there he was close to exhaustion, but found his way straight to Mahaprabhu, who embraced him as a long lost son.

'Krishna has freed you from the darkness of material enjoyment. Now I place you into the care of Svarupa Damodara.'

Svarupa took good care of him, feeding him with remnants from Mahaprabhu's plate, so that within a few days Raghunath had recovered his strength. He wanted to renounce all possible material comforts, finding they were a distraction from his constant meditation on Krishna. So as soon as he was fit again he told Svarupa he would prefer to beg his food outside the temple gate.

Over the coming years Raghunath reduced his sleeping and eating. First he survived by begging, then by visiting the free food kitchen, then he subsisted on leftover rice thrown out from the temple kitchens. When even the cows would not eat the decomposing rice he would wash it and eat a handful each day mixed with a little salt.

His father learned where he was, and repeatedly sent messengers with money, begging him to look after himself. But Raghunath was utterly disinterested in any form of comfort, even eating and sleeping. All were diversions from his continual prayer and meditation. Early on he asked Chaitanya for special instructions.

'Avoid ordinary talk, wear plain dress and eat simply,' said Mahaprabhu. 'Give honour to others and expect none for yourself. Always chant Krishna's name and meditate upon service to Radha and Krishna. In all this be guided by Svarupa Damodara.'

Raghunath heard these words and bowed in the dust at the Lord's feet, whereupon Chaitanya embraced him.

One day Chaitanya gave Raghunath his precious Govardhana Shila. He had carried this small stone from the sacred Govardhana Hill and prayed over it for two years. Now it became Raghunath's only possession, and he worshipped it daily as a form of Krishna.

In later years, after the Lord's disappearance, Raghunath went to Vrindavan where he lived the rest of his life beside Govardhana Hill. Each day, while subsisting on a little whey, he chanted Krishna's name for twenty-two hours and offered respects to thousands of devotees. Full of love for Mahaprabhu he devoted himself to fulfilling the instructions he was given, and expressed his feelings of gratitude and humility in beautiful Sanskrit verses:

> 'Though I am a fallen soul, lowest of men,
> Sri Chaitanya Mahaprabhu delivered me from
> the blazing forest fire of material opulence by
> his mercy. He handed me over in great pleasure
> to Svarupa Damodara, his personal associate.
> The Lord also gave me the garland of small
> conchshells that he wore on his chest and a
> stone from Govardhana Hill, although they
> were very dear to him. That same Lord Sri
> Chaitanya Mahaprabhu awakens within my
> heart and makes me mad after him.'

He wrote many poems of love for Radha and Krishna and some longer poetic works filled with his mystical visions of the spiritual realm. So it was that through the life of his dear devotee Raghunath Das Goswami, Sri Chaitanya inspired the highest standard of prayer and renunciation.

EVERY DAY CHAITANYA VISITED THE SAINTLY HARIDAS. On his way to the ocean he would stop and talk with him about Krishna. Haridas, the one who introduced Raghunath to Krishna, constantly chanted Krishna's holy names and was revered by the whole community of devotees. They gave him the name Namacharya, 'teacher of the name'.

One day Mahaprabhu thought with sadness of how people suffer in this world of birth and death. He spoke with Haridas.

'Dear Haridas, how will the fallen souls of this age ever be freed?'

'They can be freed by chanting the holy name,' assured Haridas. 'Take the example of Ajamila described in the *Srimad Bhagavatam*. He was inspired to give his youngest son the name Narayana. As an old man on the point of death he cried out his son's name, and in so doing unintentionally called the name of God, and so was liberated. When people pronounce the syllables of God's name, such as *'rama'*, even in the course of casual conversation, they are purified. Since they are not consciously calling on the name of God, their chanting is without offence. The holy name is so powerful that even a shadow of the Name can free the soul from material life.' Sri Chaitanya was consoled by Haridas's faithful words, and wanted to hear more.

'What of the animals, trees and insects who are incapable of chanting—how will they be freed?' he asked.

'They too will be saved,' replied Haridas. 'You have chanted the names loudly, and your followers also chant with you. As the holy name echoes around the world all living beings are purified. The echo that we hear is the chanting of all creation reverberating with the sacred sound. With your sankirtan movement you have set in motion the liberation of the entire universe. As old souls are liberated, new souls come to take their places, and they also hear the holy names. So there is no end to your mercy.'

All his life Haridas had followed this simple and profound teaching of the all-purifying grace of Krishna's holy name. As a young man he had experienced it for himself. He was born in a Muslim family in East Bengal, but orphaned at an early age. When he first found faith in Krishna he thought himself unqualified, on account of his Muslim upbringing, to openly worship Krishna. So he placed his full faith in Krishna's holy name and started to chant continuously. He vowed that each day he would chant three hundred thousand names, which took him all day and all night, leaving only an hour or two for sleeping and eating.

Haridas saw people suffering due to ignorance of spiritual life. While Advaita prayed in Shantipur, Haridas chanted fervently. Both of them called upon Krishna to descend into this world and teach the path of pure love for God. People revered Haridas as a saint, but the local tax collector was envious of the honour he received, and conspired to shame him. Seeing that Haridas was young and handsome, he paid a beautiful prostitute to tempt him to break his vows.

When Haridas was alone at night, the girl came to his shelter in the forest and offered herself to him, but she could not distract him from his chanting, and as long as he continued chanting her charms were rendered powerless. Through three nights she stayed beside him, waiting to be satisfied, and each morning the sun rose with not a pause in the flow of his chanting. The beautiful girl sat hearing the divine sound of Krishna's name chanted from the lips of a pure soul, and gradually her will evaporated along with the shadows of the night. By sunrise at the end of the third night she fell at his feet begging his mercy and forgiveness. Haridas, who had stayed only for her benefit, initiated her with the mantra of Krishna's names, gave her his own seat and hermit's dwelling, then left that place never to return. She stayed and chanted Krishna's names as his faithful disciple for the rest of her life. In time many people came to learn from her and also found faith in Krishna's names.

No one had ever seen such steadfastness and faith in Krishna's names as Haridas possessed, and as he moved among the villages, his reputation spread until he attracted the attention of the Muslim rulers. They feared his influence among the people. The local deputy had him imprisoned and publicly whipped in twenty-two marketplaces. But Haridas never stopped chanting, and before he passed unconscious he forgave his tormentors. Taking him for dead they threw him in the Ganges, where he floated downstream and miraculously recovered. Trusting in Krishna's shelter he reached the village of Candapura, where he was taken in by the Vaishnavas and given a hermit's cottage. Here he was daily visited by a young boy whom he taught and blessed with attachment for Krishna's holy names. This boy was the young Raghunath, who later became the great Raghunath Das Goswami.

One day a meeting was held by the local Vaishnava community. They used to meet and sing together, but people mocked their faith in Vishnu. So they called upon Haridas to speak about the power of chanting Krishna's name.

'As the rising sun drives away the ocean of darkness of this world,' declared Haridas, 'so chanting the holy name even once banishes all the effects of a person's sinful life. When the first glimmer of dawn touches the horizon, even before the sun appears, the ghosts of night flee; then as the sun appears in fullness the day begins. In the same way, the shadow of the holy name, even imperfectly chanted, brings liberation. Yet such liberation is not the full effect of the holy name. The true affect of chanting with faith and reverence is to awaken the soul's ecstatic love for Krishna. This is worth infinitely more than liberation.'

Haridas's teaching on the holy name was greatly appreciated by his audience. But there was one brahmin who took exception.

'Why must you always chant so loud? It is better to contemplate silently.'

'By chanting silently you benefit your own soul,' replied Haridas, 'Whereas by chanting aloud you purify all who hear, even those in the form of animals and even plants, who cannot chant for themselves.'

Eventually Haridas came to Shantipur, the home of Advaita Acarya, who gave him shelter in a cave by the Ganges where Haridas continued his constant flow of chanting undisturbed. Advaita was leader of the local brahmin community. He publicly honoured Haridas as an exalted soul by giving him the chief offering at the annual *sraddha* ceremony for departed souls. After this no one dared criticise Haridas for his faith in the holy name. He and Advaita became close companions and spent long hours immersed in talking about Krishna.

Nearby, in Navadvipa, momentous events were unfolding as the young Nimai Pandit, whose divine appearance they had both prayed for, began his sankirtan movement. Haridas was among the first to join the young Chaitanya. With Nityananda he went out preaching door to door, and led one of the three groups of chanters that encircled the Kazi's house. When Sri Chaitanya became a sannyasi and moved to Jagannath Puri, it was not long before Haridas followed him there. By this time Haridas was in advanced age, and Mahaprabhu respected him as his teacher and mentor. The fact that Haridas was a former Muslim gave him special significance: he showed the universality of surrender to Krishna's names. So long as Haridas was there in Puri faithfully chanting, he was a beacon of hope for ordinary people, showing how all that really mattered was devotion to chanting Krishna's holy name.

So it was that, without fail, Sri Chaitanya visited Haridas every day.

13

ENGULFING OCEAN OF LOVE

WITH THE PASSAGE OF TIME the devotees in Bengal never forgot Mahaprabhu. He was their life and soul. When he left them and moved to Puri they couldn't get over the loss, just as the gopis of Vrindavan never got over their loss of Krishna. Consequently each year they went on pilgrimage to see him in Puri and stayed from the Rathayatra festival in June until the end of September.

Travelling was risky, for there were bandits in some parts, and the borders between the warring kingdoms of Bengal and Orissa were well-guarded. There were taxes and tolls to pay, and rivers and estuaries to navigate through the coastal lands of the Bay of Bengal. Guiding a group of two hundred or more pilgrims over the distance of three hundred miles needed careful organisation. This responsibility was taken on by a physician named Shivananda Sena, who knew the roads well. He collected financial contributions, arranged meals and lodgings, and paid tolls and boat charges.

Each year the group carried gifts for Mahaprabhu, among which were three large bags of sweets and savouries. This custom was started by Raghava Pandit and his sister Damayanti, who lived in Panihati. They were expert cooks who had many times received Mahaprabhu in their home, where they enjoyed a special relationship with him based on their beautifully cooked offerings. Mahaprabhu kept their bags with him all year, tasting something each day and sharing it with his guests, so remembering the love of his devotees in Navadvipa.

One year Shivananda adopted a stray dog as one of the party. The Vaishnavas welcomed the dog as a fellow soul, a servant of Krishna, and the dog followed them everywhere. Shivananda even paid the ferrymen extra to take the dog on their boats with them. One evening he was detained and no one remembered to feed the animal. As a consequence, next morning the dog was nowhere to be seen. They spent a long time searching, but in the end had to continue their journey without their faithful friend.

The party arrived in Puri just as Mahaprabhu and his friends were setting off for the lake called Narendra Sarovara, where an annual water festival was held for the temple deities of Krishna and Balarama. They joined together to sing and dance their way to the lakeside. The men plunged into the water with Mahaprabhu, Nityananda and Advaita in their midst and began splashing and fighting like children. Time stood still as a spiritual ecstasy descended upon the scene.

They felt they had entered the eternal pastimes of Vrindavan, in which the cowherd boys played with Krishna in the Yamuna. Floating in an ocean of joy, they called the names of Krishna and Chaitanya, laughing and crying, while on the shore others danced and sang the holy names.

After enjoying themselves in the water they dressed and followed Mahaprabhu to the great temple to see Jagannath. Each time Mahaprabhu looked at Jagannath he felt he was seeing him for the first time. He gazed at the deity's big black eyes and encompassing smile, and was unable to restrain his tears. Beside him the devotees' hearts melted and they also wept. They saw their two Lords together: the Jagannath who stood still in the temple, and the Jagannath who moved among them sharing his love. They felt as if Jagannath, attracted by the sound of their singing his names, had come in person to chant alongside them.

The next morning the pilgrims from Bengal went to visit Mahaprabhu in his rooms and were amazed to find their lost fellow pilgrim, the dog, sitting on the terrace happily chewing coconut pulp fed to him by Mahaprabhu from his own hand.

'This animal has the highest good fortune,' they exclaimed. 'Eating the remnants of Mahaprabhu's plate bestows love for God.' They were truly astonished, however, at what happened next.

'Chant the holy name of Krishna!' laughed Mahaprabhu addressing the dog.

'Krishna! Krishna!' barked the dog.

In amazement and thankfulness Shivananda bowed his head to the ground before the dog, begging forgiveness for his neglect. The next day the dog could not be found, and all guessed the fortunate creature had left this world, liberated by Mahaprabhu's mercy.

Whenever the devotees arrived from Bengal they gathered for a huge kirtan. Mahaprabhu divided them into seven groups, each with a principal dancer. Then mystically he entered each group, appearing in seven places at once. With drums beating and cymbals resounding, the devotees felt they were swimming in a sea of love.

'My head falls at the feet of Jagannath,' sang Mahaprabhu over and over again.

Sometimes he fell unconscious on the ground, then rising again his body would be shaken by ecstasies, trembling like a leaf in the wind.

Crowds of onlookers, including the King and his queens, heard the sound of the chanting pierce the air like shimmering thunder, causing everyone's hair to stand on end. No one noticed the passage of time as the chanters drank in Mahaprabhu's love.

Then Nityananda, seeing that it was late afternoon and everyone was exhausted, called a halt, and they went with Mahaprabhu to bathe in the ocean and eat together by the seashore.

The visiting devotees settled in their various sleeping quarters as arranged by Sivananda Sena, and one by one went to meet Mahaprabhu. Some were his old friends who had known him since childhood. There was the sweet-maker Paramesvara, whose home as a little boy Chaitanya used to visit and be given sweets whenever he came. Now the elderly man came to see him.

'Paramesvara, how good to see you after all these years,' said Mahaprabhu and asked after his family. Such simple exchanges filled the devotees' hearts with happiness. Just to see Sri Chaitanya and be ackowledged by him was their greatest satisfaction.

'You go through so much difficulty to come here, leaving your homes and families to make a dangerous journey. I should stop you, but then I would miss you too much. I am a mendicant with no money. How can I repay you for coming to see me year after year? I have only this body. This I give to you. You may do with me as you wish.'

Every day Mahaprabhu went to a different house for lunch, invited by one of his devotees from Bengal as they each took their turn to please him personally. One year, when Advaita Acarya's turn came, he and his wife Sita began to cook their Lord's favourite preparations in great anticipation. When Advaita cooked his whole being would be absorbed in his task to make the best food possible for his Lord. But on this occasion he was distracted by the thought that Mahaprabhu would not come alone: he would probably bring with him a crowd of sannyasis so that Advaita and Sita would not have the treasured chance to be alone with their beloved Lord.

While he was immersed in his cooking and wondering how many would accompany his Lord, a tropical storm suddenly arose. The sky turned dark, lightning flashed and thunder rolled, a storm of hail swept the landscape followed by torrential rain and high winds. The sannyasis who were expected to join Mahaprabhu at Advaita's house gave up their plans and stayed under shelter. Advaita guessed no one would come and in disappointment began to make a mental offering of the completed dishes with prayers to Mahaprabhu. In meditation he called him to come and eat.

'Hare Krishna,' came a voice from the door.

Advaita turned and saw his Lord enter the room, untouched by raging storm or torrential rain. Filled with joy he gave his master a seat and washed his feet. Then he and Sita fulfilled their cherished desires, serving him each preparation until he had eaten everything they had cooked.

'No one cooks as sweetly as you two,' said he, as Advaita and Sita radiated happiness.

'Dear Lord, please never leave us,' they prayed. 'Let us serve you eternally.'

When the time came for the devotees to return to Bengal, each year their parting became more difficult. One year, before they left, Mahaprabhu spoke earnestly with Nityananda.

'In the past I have asked you to remain in Bengal all year round, but still you come to see me. I know you come out of love, but I have a special request: please do not come again. Stay in Bengal and I will be with you there.'

From that time Nityananda remained in Bengal and served his dear brother from a distance. He showed his own dazzling style in the mood of Balarama, and drew people to Krishna wherever he went, performing vibrant kirtans that enchanted the people of the villages. Always he spoke of Chaitanya as his master, and as he danced and sang with infectious joy of love for God the people came to love him as they loved Chaitanya. He was their link to him. Whenever they saw Nitai their hearts filled with the same joy as if he were Nimai, and their love for Krishna increased.

But there were some in Bengal who did not appreciate Nityananda's carefree ways. Among them was a brahmin of Navadvipa who in his youth had been a student of Nimai Pandit, and was now a faithful devotee of Chaitanya Mahaprabhu. When he saw Nityananda's behaviour he was doubtful. How could such an unconventional person represent Sri Chaitanya, he thought? This doubt preyed on his mind, so he left for Jagannath Puri. Every day he visited Mahaprabhu and sat at his feet, until one day, finding they were alone together, he placed his doubt before his master.

'Nityananda wanders around Navadvipa wearing golden ornaments and brightly-coloured silk clothing. I cannot understand why he does this. He chews intoxicating betel nuts and disregards all conventions. People say he is a great soul, but why then does he not behave as a renunciant should? My heart is filled with this doubt. If you think I can understand, please tell me the truth about him.'

Mahaprabhu appreciated the good intentions of his devotee, who asked with honesty and a genuine desire to deepen his faith, so he answered him carefully.

'I assure you that Nityananda is untouched by fault, as a lotus leaf is untouched by water. Do you not know what Krishna says in the *Srimad Bhagavatam*: "My pure devotees have neither faults nor virtues because they have attained me, who am above all material concepts."

'Furthermore Krishna says, "If you find fault with my devotee, even though you worship me and chant my name, you will find many obstacles in your path. On the other hand, if you love my devotee, you will certainly attain me."

'So I say that anyone who criticises Nityananda will not make spiritual progress. Even if you see Nityananda in a wine-shop with a girl on his arm, still you are to worship him. If you love him, you love me. This is the truth.'

When he heard these words spoken by his master, the brahmin found his doubts left him. Faith in Nityananda arose in his heart. Peacefully he returned to Navadvipa, where he went to Nityananda and submitted to him. He was shown great mercy, as were all who sought Nitai's help.

SIX YEARS PASSED. The annual visits from Bengal came to an end. Mahaprabhu was now thirty-six years old, and more and more he withdrew from the world. The only ones he wanted to spend time with were a small circle of intimate companions, including Svarupa Damodara and Ramananda.

From the time he first arrived in Puri, it was his custom every day to visit the deity of Jagannath. Remembering that first occasion, when he had upset the temple attendants by falling unconscious on the floor in front of Jagannath, he always stayed at the back of the temple so as not to disturb anyone. He stood beside the column that supported the form of Vishnu's eagle carrier Garuda, who knelt with folded hands ready to serve his Lord.

This was Mahaprabhu's recognised place, where he would always be found when he was in the temple. From here he gazed at Jagannath, sometimes in a trance, unaware of his surroundings. As he looked upon Jagannath he saw only Krishna playing his flute in Vrindavan. Tears would pour from his lotus eyes and collect in the depression at the foot of the column. When eventually he withdrew his gaze, he felt bereft.

'Where has Krishna gone?' He would ask despairingly of those nearby. 'Where is Vrindavan? Where is that beautiful cowherd who plays the flute?'

At times such as these, swept by waves of emotion, he lost all sense of time and place. As he became ever more absorbed in his love for Krishna, he survived by the care of friends, those fortunate souls gathered close around him.

His faithful servant Govinda many times protected him when he was lost in another dimension. Once when he was in the temple beside Garuda's pillar, a woman, unaware of her actions, scrambled onto his shoulders to better see Jagannath. Mesmerised by his own sight of Jagannath, he paid her no attention. It was his faithful servant Govinda who persuaded her to come down. On another occasion he heard someone singing a love song to Krishna and ran toward the source, intending to embrace the singer.

'It is a woman singing!' cried Govinda.

'Dear Govinda, you saved my life,' said Mahaprabhu, halting in his tracks. 'If I had embraced a woman I should have died.'

From that day, Govinda stayed always at his side and tended to his every need. Once after a long kirtan Mahaprabhu and the devotees bathed in the sea then had lunch before their afternoon rest. When he reached his room he was so exhausted from his dancing that he dropped to the floor and fell fast asleep, right in the doorway. Govinda came to massage his legs but found the doorway blocked by his master's sleeping form. He asked him to move aside but heard only a murmur.

'I am too tired to move.'

'Unless you move I can't massage your feet,' said Govinda.

'Do as you wish—I cannot move.'

Govinda thought it would be disrespectful for him to step over his master's body, but without doing so he could not serve him. So carefully he stepped over him and massaged his feet. When he had finished, instead of leaving to eat his lunch, he sat and waited. After some time Mahaprabhu woke up.

'You are still here? Why did you not go to eat?'

'Because you are blocking the door.'

'You could have left by the same way you came in.'

Govinda said nothing, but thought to himself, 'I will commit a hundred offenses to serve you, my Lord, but none to serve myself.'

Jagadananda was an intimate friend of Mahaprabhu, whose relationship with his Lord was sometimes stormy on account of his intense love for him. He had been with Mahaprabhu since the early days in Navadvipa, and followed him to Puri.

Once Jagadananda brought a large clay pitcher of sandalwood oil for Mahaprabhu, transported with great care all the way from Navadvipa. He gave it to Govinda and asked him to use a little every day for his master's massage. But the oil was perfumed and Mahaprabhu refused to use it.

'When people smell this perfume on my body they will think me one of those false sannyasis that keeps women,' he told Govinda. 'Give it to the temple to be used in the lamps on Jagannath's altar, then Jagadananda's labours will be put to good use.'

Jagadananda heard from Govinda that his gift had not been accepted. He came straight to see Mahaprabhu, and was about to speak when his master spoke first.

'I appreciate your gift, Jagadananda, bringing this oil all the way from Bengal, but I am a sannyasi and I cannot accept it. Please give it to the temple for the service of Jagannath's lamps, that will be a good use for it.'

Tears sprang to Jagadananda's eyes.

'Who told you this?' he burst out. 'I never brought oil from Bengal.' Saying this he heaved the clay jug into the courtyard where it smashed to the ground and shattered into a thousand pieces. After this he ran off and locked himself in his room where he fasted and refused all entreaties to come out.

After three days Mahaprabhu came and spoke to him.

'Jagadananda!' he called through the door. 'I want you to cook for me today. I am going to the temple and will be back at noon.'

Jagadananda got up and bathed. He felt better now. By the time Mahaprabhu returned, with the help of his friends he had cooked a feast. He washed his Lord's feet and placed a banana leaf before him, piled high with many kinds of vegetable preparations.

'I will not eat alone, Jagadananda. Make another place for yourself and join me.'

'I will eat as soon as I have served you, Lord,' replied Jagadananda, so Mahaprabhu agreed to eat first. Jagadananda made him eat from everything he had cooked, and though it was enough for many servings Mahaprabhu dared not refuse whatever he offered. At last he finished, and asked Jagadananda to sit down and eat. But Jagadananda again excused himself, saying he must first serve the others who had helped cook.

'Please go with Govinda for your massage, then have your rest. Don't worry about me—I will eat later.'

Mahaprabhu left, but he would not rest until he heard that Jagadananda had finally eaten.

SRI CHAITANYA REMAINED in Jagannath Puri experiencing transcendental ecstasies with his devotees. During the day they gathered to sing and dance, and visit Jagannath in the temple. At night, with a small group of intimate companions including Svarupa Damodara and Ramananda Raya, Mahaprabhu heard about Krishna, the beautiful cowherd boy of Vrindavan. Absorbed in songs of Chandidas, poems of Vidyapati, Jayadeva's *Gita Govinda*, and stories from the *Srimad Bhagavatam*, he tasted from the endless ocean of love for Krishna.

Haridas was now an elderly man. Each day Govinda took him sacred food from Jagannath's offering in the big temple. One day when Govinda arrived he found Haridas lying on his back hardly able to vibrate Krishna's names. With great effort Haridas took a small portion of Jagannath's prasadam, then said he would fast, since on the previous day he had been unable to complete his fixed number of holy names. Govinda hurried back to tell Mahaprabhu of Haridas's condition.

The following day Mahaprabhu came and asked Haridas how he was.

'My body is well, Lord, but my mind is disturbed, for I cannot complete my chanting.'

'Now that you are old you can reduce your daily quota,' his Master assured him. 'You have already achieved all you were sent into this world to do, for you have taught everyone the glories of the holy names of Krishna.'

Haridas had a special plea.

'I am the lowest of men, yet you rescued me and allowed me to be your servant. You blessed me and made me dance in so many ways. Now, Lord, I have one remaining desire. I foresee that soon you will leave this world. I do not wish to see that closing chapter. Let me leave this life in your presence, gazing into your moonlike face, with your lotus feet upon my heart while I chant your holy name.'

'My dear Haridas, if this is your desire then surely Krishna will fulfil it. But how can I continue to live if you go from here and leave me behind?'

'Lord, I am insignificant among your dazzling associates,' murmured Haridas. 'If an ant dies, what is the loss?'

Hearing these words Mahaprabhu embraced him.

Promising to return the next day, he left to bathe in the ocean and say his noon prayers. The following morning he brought with him a group of devotees and they surrounded Haridas.

'What news, Haridas?' he asked.

'My Lord, whatever mercy you can give me,' murmured Haridas.

With this, the Master began to chant Krishna's names and all the devotees joined him, encircling Haridas and singing with deep fervour. As they chanted, Sri Chaitanya recited the glories of Haridas Thakur as the great teacher of the Holy Name. While he spoke, Haridas grasped Mahaprabhu's feet and held them to his chest. He fixed his eyes upon his master's shining face and chanted Krishna's names with renewed strength, tears running down his cheeks. Even as he chanted, he gave up his life in front of everyone.

The chanting increased in intensity as Sri Chaitanya raised Haridas's body, which weighed almost nothing, and danced with it down to the sea. There they bathed the body of Haridas Thakur, and with gentle care interred it in a grave near the shore, digging with their bare hands in the sand. In the grave they placed sacred remnants from Jagannath, and Chaitanya with his own hands threw sand onto Haridas's body. They made a platform over the place, protected by fencing, and danced and sang around it in ecstasy. Then they bathed in the sea and Mahaprabhu led them in observing a festival in the town. He asked the shopkeepers to contribute ingredients, and a great feast was prepared. Mahaprabhu personally served the food. He then announced a benediction.

'Whoever has witnessed this festival of the passing of Haridas Thakur will soon achieve Krishna. Such is the power of seeing Haridas. Krishna was merciful to me, and gave me his company. Now, being independent, Krishna has broken that companionship. Haridas has left by his own will, and I had no power to keep him. Without him this world has lost a great jewel.'

Saying farewell to the devotees, Sri Chaitanya left to rest, his heart filled with both joy and sorrow.

SRI CHAITANYA HAD A DREAM of Krishna dancing with the gopis. Krishna played his flute, standing artfully curved three ways. Wearing yellow and garlanded with forest flowers, He danced with Radha in the midst of a circle of gopis. Seeing this intoxicating vision Mahaprabhu felt he was at last in Vrindavan.

Then Govinda woke him, and Krishna vanished. Devastated, he sat alone on the ground, tracing patterns in the sand with his nails.

'I found Krishna, Lord of Vrindavan, but I have lost him again,' he cried, blinded by tears. 'Who has taken my Krishna? Where is Vrindavan, and what is this place I have come to?'

Unable to recover his peace of mind, he spent the day mechanically going through his routine—bathing, visiting the temple, and taking his midday meal. Only when evening came could he reveal his state of confusion to his dearmost friends, Ramananda Raya and Svarupa Damodara.

> 'My mind has left me and gone to Vrindavan as a beggar, taking my senses as his disciples. He wears a fabulous earring, the ring of Krishna's rasa dance with the gopis, and his alms bowl is carved from my hopes. His body, smeared with ashes, is covered with the cloth of anxiety, he is emaciated from fasting, and his only words are, "Alas! Krishna!" He wanders through the forest of Vrindavan eating herbs and roots, which are the sweet remnants left behind by the gopis from their play with Krishna. At night he sits awake, hoping to see Krishna dancing, but he is unable to find Him. Thus my mind has deserted me and I am left in trance.'

His friends tried to calm him by singing verses from *Gita Govinda* and other Vaishnava poems. Late that night they persuaded him to lie down in his room, and went to their beds. Outside his door slept Govinda, and all three doors to his room were bolted so he would not wander out into the night.

Mahaprabhu lay awake, unable to sleep. Loudly he called on Krishna's names, the sound of his voice vibrating through the house. In the small hours Svarupa awoke and heard that all was quiet. He went to look in on his master but found the room empty. He could not understand how this could be, because the doors were still locked. Dismayed, he woke the others, and fearing for their Lord's safety they went in search of him through the darkened streets of Puri. At last they found him lying in the road beside the main gate to the Jagannath temple.

In relief they gathered round, but when they saw his condition their fears increased. He was unconscious, his skin cool to touch, and he did not appear to be breathing. Furthermore his body was strangely elongated, his limbs distended at the joints.

Not daring to touch him the devotees simply began to chant loudly. All at once Mahaprabhu's eyes opened and his body regained its normal form. He sat up and recognised Svarupa bending over him.

'Where am I? How did I come here?' he asked.

'Let us take you home and I will tell you everything,' urged Svarupa gently.

Dazed, he allowed himself to be helped to his room, where Svarupa told him all that had happened.

'I remember none of this,' he said. 'All I know is that I saw Krishna, for an instant only, then he was gone. Like a flash of lightning, Krishna appeared and disappeared.'

Sri Chaitanya spent his days in and out of external awareness. He was sometimes able to carry on his normal activities, but the least stimulus could trigger a sudden change. Once, when he went to the temple to see Jagannath, he was transfixed with the realization that Jagannath was Krishna himself. He heard Krishna's playful words and the sound of Krishna's flute; felt the cool touch of Krishna's body; smelled the musk that Krishna always wore; and tasted the sweetness of Krishna's lips. All these sensations fought for his attention at once. Unable to steady himself he fainted and had to be helped home. That night he tried to explain his experiences to Svarupa and Ramananda.

'My mind is like a horse ridden by five riders. It cannot resist Krishna's beauty, the sound of his voice, his touch, his fragrance or the taste of his lips. Each of my senses pulls in a different direction. All at once my mind is lost, and I feel I am going to die.'

Clinging to the necks of his two friends he begged them, 'What shall I do? Where shall I go? Tell me how I can find Krishna.'

One day as he walked on the beach he saw a beautiful garden and mistook it for Vrindavan forest. Running into the garden he searched for Krishna, in the same way the gopis searched in the forest after Krishna disappeared from their *rasa* dance. Absorbed in the mood of the gopis, he spoke to the trees and creepers.

'Have you seen Krishna? Did he pass this way?' Wandering here and there, he chanted verses from the songs of the gopis in the forest. Ecstasies of anxiety, humility, anger and impatience shook his body, like elephants fighting in a sugarcane field. Tossed this way and that, suddenly he saw Krishna in front of him, standing beneath a kadamba tree and playing his flute. At once he fell to the ground unconscious. His friends came and took him on their laps. Chanting to him and massaging his feet, they brought him back to external awareness.

'Where has Krishna gone? I saw him, but now I have lost him,' he cried when he opened his eyes. Svarupa could only comfort him with verses from his favourite poems about Krishna, and they brought him home.

IT WAS THE AUTUMN FULL MOON NIGHT of the Sarat season, the same moon under which Krishna danced all night with the gopis in Vrindavan. Mahaprabhu walked with his friends along the seashore. Many times they had visited here over the years, yet this night brought special memories. As he passed through the gardens along the seashore, Sri Chaitanya was immersed in thoughts of Vrindavan. Different ecstatic emotions took hold of him. He was alternately stunned, trembling, perspiring, turning pale and weeping; he laughed with joy, he cried, he danced and sang, he ran here and there, and sometimes he fainted in the sand.

By his side Svarupa Damodara, singing of Krishna, came to a verse telling how after the *rasa* dance Krishna and the gopis bathed in the waters of the Yamuna River. At that moment Mahaprabhu saw the waves of the ocean reflecting the light of the full moon. Unnoticed by anyone, moving with the speed of mind, he dove headlong into the waves, thinking them to be the Yamuna River. He floated away unconscious into the darkness before anyone had missed him. The ocean currents carried him northwards along the coast, far from Puri. Under the moonlight, deep in trance he drifted silently among the waves.

As soon as his disappearance was noticed, anxiety swept his friends. Some ran toward the temple, others searched the town, some looked in the seafront gardens, others went as far as the Gundica temple. Eventually they all returned to the beach. Their hopes of finding him began to fade. They imagined a disaster had taken place, that they would never see him again.

Just then, as they searched along the seashore in the darkness, a fisherman came out of the night. He was laughing, crying, dancing and repeatedly singing the name 'Hari!' When they spoke to him they saw he was shaking with fear.

'Why are you acting like this? What have you seen?'

'I caught a dead body in my net,' the fisherman stammered. 'At first I thought it a big fish, but then I saw it was a human body, and tried to release it back into the water. Accidentally I touched it and now a ghost has entered me, making me mad. I cannot stop shivering and crying.'

'Tell us more. What did this body look like?'

'It was very long, with extended limbs loosened at the joints. Sometimes it seemed to open its eyes and make a murmuring sound. I am frightened to go back there.'

Svarupa assured the fisherman there was nothing to fear and persuaded him to lead them to the place where he had left the body. There they found Mahaprabhu sprawled on the shore in a frightening condition, his elongated body bleached white by the sea and covered in sand. Carefully they wiped him clean and laid him on a fresh cloth. They gathered round and chanted loudly. For a long time they continued to sing and nothing happened. Suddenly he opened his eyes, stirred and stood up. His body seemed recovered, but although he was alert he was unaware of his surroundings.

'I went to Vrindavan and saw the River Yamuna,' he said, hardly seeing his companions. 'There I watched Krishna sport with the gopis in the water. The gopis, dressed in white, were like lightning, and Krishna was dark like a raincloud. They showered water upon each other, fought hand to hand, face to face, chest to chest, teeth to teeth and nail to nail. I saw thousands of gopis, and thousands of Krishnas. Srimati Radharani was there and Krishna captured her. He took her into the deep water where she clung to his neck to save herself, and floated like a lotus flower. Then Krishna quarrelled with her, and the gopis closed around to give her protection. They looked like a cluster of white lotus flowers.

'When this play was over the gopis arranged a picnic on the riverbank, where a small jewelled house stood among the trees and creepers. They served Krishna wonderful varieties of fruits and sweets cooked by Radharani. When he had eaten, and when Radha and the gopis had tasted his remnants, he lay down with Radha in the jewelled house, fanned by the gopis. Then everyone fell asleep. I saw all this and my mind was saturated with peace. All of a sudden a great noise brought me back here. Now I have lost Vrindavan and the Yamuna, and I don't know where Krishna and the gopis have gone.'

As dawn was breaking Svarupa gently consoled Sri Chaitanya and told him how while he had been in ecstasy they had been in agony, and had searched for him all night long. Submissively, their beloved master allowed them to bathe him in the sea and take him home.

EVERY YEAR JAGADANANDA VISITED Mahaprabhu's mother in Navadvipa with news and gifts from her son. Many years had passed since mother and son had seen each other. This year Jagadananda brought her a poignant message.

'Mother, when I gave up your service to become a sannyasi I broke my religious principles, and because of this I have become mad. You told me to stay in Jagannath Puri, and here I must remain till the end of my life. Please forgive me, for I depend on you always.'

When Advaita heard this message he recited a mysterious poem for Mahaprabhu. Jagadananda memorised it and on his return repeated it to his Lord:

'Tell Sri Chaitanya Mahaprabhu we have all become mad like him. Say there is no more demand for rice in the marketplace. Say that all of us who are mad have lost interest in the material world. This message comes from one who has also become mad.'

Mahaprabhu smiled. 'This is Advaita's order to me.'
Svarupa asked the meaning of the poem.

'Advaita Acarya is expert in the art of worship. He invites the Deity to come and receive worship, then when the worship is complete he sends the Deity away. I do not understand his words, for he is a great mystic.'

As he pondered Advaita's message, Mahaprabhu's thoughts turned to Krishna leaving Vrindavan on the occasion when the gopis surrounded his chariot and pleaded with him to stay. After Krishna had left, Radha spoke to her friend Visakha in despair. Mahaprabhu now spoke her words, clinging to Ramananda Raya and speaking to Svarupa Damodara as if he were a gopi friend.

'My dear friend, where is Krishna, who rises like the moon from the ocean of Nanda Maharaja? Where is Krishna, whose head is decorated with a peacock feather? Where is Krishna, whose flute vibrates such a deep sound, who is so expert in dancing the rasa dance? He is the only one who can save my life. Please tell me where I can find Krishna. My heart breaks at not seeing his face even for a moment. Show him to me now, or else

*I will die. Providence, you are so cruel! First you show
me Krishna's beautiful face and captivate my eyes, then
after only a moment you take him away.'*

Svarupa and Ramananda did their best to calm their beloved
Lord. They sang to him of the gopis meeting Krishna and
enjoying his company. Soothed by these thoughts, but still
unhappy, he was persuaded to lie down for the night, with
Svarupa and Govinda sleeping outside his door to safeguard
him. During the night they could hear him chanting as
thoughts of separation from Krishna drove him wild. He
tried to leave the room, but could not, because they had
bolted the doors. He threw himself against the walls, hurting
his tender face and body. Svarupa, woken by his cries of
distress, lit a lamp and went in to see him. When he saw the
marks on his body, his face bruised and tearful, he was filled
with deep sorrow.

'What have you done to yourself?' he said gently, soothing
him and taking him back to his bed. At such times Svarupa
remembered a verse from the poem *Krishna-Karnamrita*,
often recited by Sri Chaitanya.

> *'Because I have not met you, my days and nights
> have become unbearable. They are not passing and
> it is difficult for me to know how to live through all
> this time. Kindly let me see you, for I am in a
> precarious position.'*

In this and many ways, from the day he received Advaita's message, Mahaprabhu's ecstasies and feelings of separation from Krishna deepened. He became inconsolable. Day and night he could not rest, tossed on the endless waves of the ocean of love.

In between his drawn out ecstasies, in the lucid moments that Svarupa called external consciousness, Sri Chaitanya confided his deep spiritual convictions to his two companions. During his life he used to sing eight favourite verses to guide and inspire Krishna's devotees on the spiritual path. Now he repeated these verses, elaborating on their deep meaning. They came to be known as *Sikshastaka*, eight verses of instruction.

'My friends, chanting God's names is the best spiritual practice in this Age of Kali. Hear me when I say...'

I

Glory to the chanting of Krishna's name,
which cleanses the dust of years from the mirror
of the heart, extinguishes the blazing fire of birth
and death, spreads the shining moon of good
fortune and inspires true wisdom. This chanting
expands the ocean of bliss, and gives all who
bathe in that ocean a taste of sweetest nectar at
every step.

'Chanting banishes the cycle of sinful life and cleanses the heart. It awakens one's desire to serve Krishna and brings spiritual bliss. Through chanting one achieves Krishna's company and the opportunity to serve Him. This service is like an ocean of love.'

In humility and gratitude, Sri Chaitanya felt he had no love for Krishna's holy name. He recited a second verse:

2

O my Lord, your many names possess all
your personal potencies, and there are no limits
for how or when to chant them. Your mercy
upon me is so great, yet my misfortune is such
that I have no attraction for your names.

'Because different people desire different things,
the Lord has given many different names for us to
chant. Regardless of time or place, one can chant
in any way, and so achieve all perfection. Now I will
tell you the best way to chant.'

3

One who feels lower than the grass, who is
more tolerant than a tree, who expects no
personal honour, yet gives all honour to others—
can easily chant the name of the Lord constantly.

'When a tree is mistreated it still gives fruit and shelter, without protesting or even asking for water. So a humble Vaishnava, who knows that Krishna lives in all beings, gives respect to them all and asks for nothing. If one chants in this mood one will certainly awaken one's love for God.'

As he spoke, Mahaprabhu's own humility grew, and he prayed for the gift of service:

4

I have no desire to enjoy wealth, fame or a beautiful partner. What I want, O almighty Lord, is that I may have your causeless devotional service in my life—birth after birth.

5

O Krishna, I am your eternal servant, but
somehow I have fallen into this ocean of birth
and death. Please be merciful and place me as a
particle of dust at your lotus feet.

Saying these prayers in deep humility,
Mahaprabhu longed to chant Krishna's name in
ecstatic love. He continued:

6

*When will tears stream from my eyes, words
falter in my throat, and the hairs of my body
stand on end by chanting your name?*

Overcome with feelings of separation from
Krishna, he began to lose his peace of mind. In
distress he recited a seventh verse:

7

A moment seems to be a thousand years, tears flow from my eyes like torrents of rain, all the world appears empty without you, Govinda.

He remembered Radha's words, 'A day never ends, my eyes are like clouds in the monsoon, I feel I am burning in a slow fire. Krishna ignores me just to test my love, and my friends say I should forget Him—but I cannot.'

Absorbed in Radharani's mood he spoke his heart:

8

Let Krishna embrace this servant as I fall at his feet, or let Him trample me beneath Him, or even break my heart by leaving me. He is free to do anything and everything, for He will always be the Lord of my heart, unconditionally.

Mahaprabhu was overwhelmed by Radharani's ecstasies of pure love for Krishna. As he entered deeper and deeper into her conflicting emotions his mind became unsteady. So he passed his time like a mad person in the company of his two friends, who consoled him with songs of love for Krishna.

A S A SANNYASI he traveled and preached for six years. In Jagannath Puri for a further six years he shared his love for Krishna with his followers by chanting Krishna's names. For the last twelve years of his life he experienced separation from Krishna day and night, crying and speaking in ecstasy. After twelve years of this constant rapture of love he could no longer sustain body and mind. In 1534, at the age of forty-eight, he disappeared from this world. Some say he was swept out to sea, others say he merged into the form of the deity of Tota Gopinath worshiped by his dearmost friend Gadadhara. Whatever the truth, he left no earthly remains.

Sri Chaitanya Mahaprabhu left behind a network of pure devotees of Krishna in whom his memory and teachings live on, and he left eight verses called *Sikshastaka*. These verses enshrine the highest spiritual truths and embody all that Sri Krishna Chaitanya lived and taught. Wherever his words are remembered and his name is sung, he lives on.

This was his promise:

'You, my dear devotees, are with me birth after birth.
I will never leave you, even for a moment.'

Hare Krishna Hare Krishna
Krishna Krishna Hare Hare
Hare Rama Hare Rama
Rama Rama Hare Hare

Completed in final form in Glastonbury, Somerset,
on Full Moon, Saradiya Rasayatra, 20 October 2021

First manuscript completed in Harbertonford, Devon,
on the festival of Lord Narasingha, 3 May 2004

A NOTE ON FURTHER READING

To learn more about Sri Chaitanya I recommend the writings of my teacher His Divine Grace A.C. Bhaktivedanta Swami Prabhupada. To explore in depth his teachings read *Teachings of Lord Chaitanya*, (1968). This was his first complete book published in the West and is flooded with profound truths.

For the serious student wishing to explore in depth the complete story and philosophy of Lord Chaitanya, absorb yourself in the sixteenth century masterpiece of Bengali literature, *Caitanya-Caritamrita* by Krsnadasa Kaviraja, translation and commentary by Srila Prabhupada (1975). This is a multi-volume work which includes original Bengali text, word-for-word translations and verse by verse commentary.

TIMELINES

THE LIFE OF SRI CHAITANYA

1486	Birth
1496	Brother Vishvarup leaves home
1498	Father Jagannath Misra dies
1502	Marriage to Laksmidevi
1505	Death of Laksmidevi
1506	Marriage to Vishnupriya
1510	Leaves home as a sannyasi
1510	Arrives in Jagannath Puri
1511-113	Travels in South India
1515	Pilgrimage to Vrindavan
1516	Teaches Rupa and Sanatana
1516	Returns to Puri
1522	Withdraws into seclusion
1534	Passes from this world

NOTABLE CONTEMPORARIES

1440-1518	*Kabir*
1469-1539	*Guru Nanak*
1475-1564	*Michelangelo*
1483-1546	*Martin Luther*
1498-1585	*Mirabai*
1491-1547	*Henry VIII*
1491-1556	*Ignatius of Loyola*
1508-1556	*Humayun, Mughal Emperoror of Delhi*
1515-1582	*Teresa of Avila*
1533-1603	*Queen Elizabeth I*

GLOSSARY OF NAMES

IN NAVADVIPA-BENGAL

Advaita Acharya	he who prepared the way, prayed for Chaitanya to come. Elder Vaishnava and companion of Chaitanya. One of the *Pancha Tattva*
Anupama	brother of Rupa and Sanatana
Brahmananda	close companion of Chaitanya
Chandrasekhara	close companion of Chaitanya
Digvijaya	a proud pandit
Duhkhi/Sukhi	a maid in the house of Shrivas
Gadadhara	close companion of Chaitanya, like a second brother. One of the *Pancha Tattva*
Gangadas Pandit	teacher of the young Nimai
Haridas Thakur	humble servant and close companion of Chaitanya. Chanter of the holy names
Isvara Puri	Vaishnava sannyasi and guru of Chaitanya
Jagai	lowly thief saved by Nityananda's mercy. Brother of Madhai
Jagannath Misra	father of Chaitanya and Vishvarup
Chand Kazi	Muslim governor who disapproved of Vaishnava traditions
Kesava Bharati	elderly monk who initiated Chaitanya into the order of sannyasa
Laksmidevi	Chaitanya's first wife
Madhai	lowly thief saved by Nityananda's mercy. Brother of Jagai
Mukunda	close companion of Chaitanya. Singer of songs
Murari Gupta	school-friend and student of Nimai
Nawab Husain Shah	Muslim governor of Bengal, at war with Orissa
Nityananda (Nitai)	like a brother to Chaitanya, who protected him and went on to spread his message far and wide. One of the *Pancha Tattva*
Raghunatha	young householder who renounced all to become one of Chaitanya's closest disciples and wrote many books. His wealthy father was a friend of Advaita Acharya
Rupa (Goswami)	brother of Sanatan. Senior member of Bengal government, became a disciple of Chaitanya and went on to write many books such as: Vidagdha-Madhava, Lalita-Madhava, Bhakti Rasamrita Sindhu

Saci   mother of Chaitanya and Vishvarup

Sanatan (Goswami)   brother of Rupa. Senior member of Bengal government, became a disciple of Chaitanya and went on to write several books: Brihad Bhagavatamrita, Hari Bhakti Vilasa

Shrivas   a pure devotee of Navadvip, who held regular prayer meetings in his house. One of the *Pancha Tattva*

Sita   wife of Advaita Acharya

Vishnupriya   Chaitanya's second wife

Vishvarup   Chaitanya's older brother who left home to become a sannyasi

IN VARANASI

Chandrasekhara   friend of Tapana Misra

Prakasananda   leader of the mayavadis in Varanasi

Tapana Misra   seeker of truth, the first to receive Nimai's spiritual teachings in Bengal, later moved to Varanasi

IN JAGANNATH PURI

Balabhadra Bhattacarya   Chaitanya's companion to Vrindavan

Gopinatha   brother-in-law to Sarvabhauma Bhattacarya

Kasi Misra   brahmin of Orissa, who gave Chaitanya shelter

Maharaja Prataparudra   King of Orissa 1497-154

Ramananda Raya   governor of Madras who became close associate of Chaitanya

Sarvabhauma Bhattacarya   respected elder of Puri and great Vedanta philosopher

Svarupa Damodara   close companion of Chaitanya, particularly in later life

TEACHERS

Madhavendra Puri   predecessor guru of Isvara Puri, guru of Chaitanya. He taught ecstatic love of Radha and Krishna as the goal of life

Shankaracarya   8th century reformer who spread the doctrine of Advaita

DIVINE BEINGS

Balarama   brother of Lord Krishna and Lord Jagannath

Brahma   Lord of creation

Hanuman   monkey servant of Lord Rama

Hari   one of the names of God, 'who vanquishes all miseries'

Jagannath   Lord of the Universe, the form of Krishna worshipped in the great temple at Puri

Laksmana	brother of Lord Rama
Laksmi	goddess of fortune
Narasingha	4th avatar of Vishnu in the form of half-man, half-lion
Radha	Lord Krishna's eternal consort in Vrindavan, revered as the Goddess of Devotion
Rama	7th avatar of Vishnu
Satyabhama	consort of Lord Krishna in Dvaraka
Shiva	Lord of Destruction, the supreme being within Shaivism
Subhadra	sister of Lord Jagannath
Sarasvati	Goddess of Learning, consort of Lord Brahma
Vishnu	Lord of All who dwells in the hearts of all beings
Vrindavan	home of Krishna
Vaishnava	a devotee of Vishnu or Krishna

GLOSSARY OF TERMS

Avatar	One who descends from the spiritual world
Advaita	'non-duality', refers to the philosophy of oneness with God
Bhagavad Gita	Holy scripture in which Krishna converses with Arjuna
Bhaktirasa	The love felt between Krishna and his devotees
Bhaktiyoga	The spiritual practice of devotional service to God
Brahmin	A priest or scholar
Dvaita	'duality', refers to the philosophy of difference between God and others
Ghat	A bathing place by the river
Gopis	Cowherd girls with a deep love for Krishna
Gundica	Temple in Puri
Japa	To chant mantra softly to oneself
Kirtan	To sing the names of God, often with musical accompaniment
Maya	Illusion of the material world
Mayavadi	One who sees all as illusion
Pandit	Vedic teacher or scholar
Rathayatra	Chariot festival of Lord Jagannath, Subhadra and Balarama
Sannyasi	A monk who has renounced worldly life
Sankirtan	Communal singing of God's names, usually in public
Srimad Bhagavatam	Holy scripture that includes the life story of Krishna

Index of Topics

other books from Fitzrovia Press by the same author:

Bhagavad Gita
Talks Between the Soul and God
translation with reflections
'Prime began this translation as a way of sharing the Gita
with his own children, and his commentary exudes a
fatherly and caring spirit.' *Publishers Weekly*
240 pages £7.99 ISBN 978-0-9561846-4-1

The Eight Elements
My Journey Through Life's Mysteries
'In the 1960s Ranchor Prime left home to find Krishna.
He has been searching through nature and the spirit ever
since. In this beautiful book the author reflects on his
journey and, one by one, introduces the reader to the eight
elements of ancient Hindu cosmology' *John Martineau*
240 pages £9.99 ISBN 978-0-9570722-1-3

Ranchor Prime is a disciple of A C Bhaktivedanta Swami.
He is an author and teacher, and lives in Glastonbury, England.

ranchor.co.uk